D0610387

Achieve
Your Goals

Strategies to
transform your life

ANDY SMITH

**LONDON, NEW YORK,
MUNICH, MELBOURNE, DELHI**

Produced for Dorling Kindersley
by **terry jeavons**&**company**

Project Editor	Sophie Collins
Project Art Editor	Terry Jeavons
Designer	Andrew Milne
Picture Researcher	Sarah Hopper
Senior Editor	Simon Tuite
Senior Art Editor	Sara Robin
Editor	Elizabeth Watson
DTP Designer	Traci Salter
Production Controller	Stuart Masheter
Executive Managing Editor	Adèle Hayward
Managing Art Editor	Karla Jennings
Art Director	Peter Luff
Publisher	Corinne Roberts
Special Photography	Adrian Turner

First American Edition, 2007

Published in the United States by DK Publishing,
375 Hudson Street, New York, NY 10014

07 08 09 10   10 9 8 7 6 5 4 3 2 1

Copyright © 2006 Dorling Kindersley Limited
Text copyright © 2006 Andy Smith

A Cataloging-in-Publication record for this book is
available from the Library of Congress.

ISBN 978-0-75662-607-5

ED245

DK books are available at special discounts for bulk
purchases for sales promotions, premiums, fund-raising, or
educational use. For details, contact: DK Publishing Special
Markets, 375 Hudson Street, New York, NY 10014 or
SpecialSales@dk.com

Contents

Introduction

How would you like your life to be different? Whether it's choosing a new career path, finding your soul mate, or getting your finances in order, most people have something about their life that they want to change.

The fact that you are reading this means that you are considering making changes. Like most people, you will have tried to make changes in your life before. You probably found that some were easier than others, and that some changes lasted while others did not. What was the difference between them?

Change will happen when you are ready and able to take the necessary steps

Almost any change is possible if you put all the factors in place to help you. First, make sure that you accept yourself. People sometimes avoid taking a realistic look at where their lives are now because they are worried about what they will find, and how they will feel about themselves as a result. Starting with an attitude of acceptance solves this problem. You can assess your current way of being objectively, without judging yourself. Second, make sure that you are clear about what you want. You can use the methods in *Achieve Your Goals* to clarify your vision of where you want to be, and to resolve any doubts and uncertainties so that you can be sure that this is what you really want. Finally, use brain-friendly methods to achieve your goal. Your mind is an amazingly powerful and complex mechanism. It will respond well to some approaches and will resist some others with all its might.

This book shows you the best ways to make your goals compelling and keep your mind motivated. It will work best if you start with the self-assessment on the following pages and work through the book from start to finish. If possible, team up with a goal-setting partner, so that you can support each other along the way. This helps because you can often gain additional insights from your partner as you talk through the exercises together, and also because when you tell another person about your goals, those goals become more real and you are more likely to carry them out. If you can't find a goal-setting partner right away, doing the exercises by yourself will still work—but you must do them, not just think them through, in order for them to be truly effective.

Assessing Your Skills

These questions are designed to get you thinking about goal-setting and may lead to new insights, whether you are an experienced goal achiever or just starting out. To get the full benefit, complete the assessment twice—once before you read the book and again after you have read it and, crucially, done the practical exercises. The more honest you are with yourself, the greater the benefits you will enjoy.

Before After

1 **When you think about the problems that you face now, what is your first instinct?**

A I blame others
B I blame myself
C I accept responsibility, and think about what I can do to change things

2 **When things don't work out the way you want them to, what is your response?**

A I feel that I have failed
B I redouble my efforts
C I ask myself what I need to learn from this result

3 **What kind of internal dialogues do you have?**

A They are critical
B They are supportive and encouraging
C I don't have internal dialogues—my "inner voice" is silent most of the time

4 **How do you feel about your current job?**

A I don't do any more than I have to
B It doesn't really suit me, but I work hard as a matter of pride
C My work is taking me closer to fulfilling my life's purpose

	Before	After

5 Which of these statements is closest to your philosophy of life?

A You're either lucky or unlucky
B People make their own luck
C Everything that happens is an opportunity to learn

6 Why is it important to you to achieve your goals?

A I haven't really thought about it
B Because I don't want to stay where I am now
C To increase the possibilities open to me

7 How do you feel about your strengths?

A I'm not really sure what they are
B They're better than most people's, but they're never good enough
C I know my strengths and am always ready to improve them

8 What is your attitude to the future?

A I try to live in the moment
B My future is planned out for the next five years
C I know where I'm going and I have many possible routes to get there

9 How clearly defined are your goals?

A Not very—they're just daydreams
B It's all written down and I will get there if it kills me
C They are clear and vivid, and I update them in the light of new information

10 How do you know when you're doing a good job?

A Other people tell me
B I just know
C When my feeling about it is confirmed by feedback from other people and objective evidence

11 **What would happen if you didn't achieve your goals?**

A Life would go on the same as usual
B I have to achieve my goals
C I expect to achieve them, but whatever happens, I will learn something valuable from it

12 **How clear are you about what is important to you?**

A I'm a bit vague
B I'm very clear—if I wasn't, anything could happen
C I am clear about what's important, even if it is sometimes fulfilled in unexpected ways

13 **How do you maintain your work/life balance?**

A It's not a problem—I do enough to get by, and then stop
B It all goes by the board when there's a deadline
C I am realistic about what I can do, and make sure the important things get done first

14 **Do you deserve to be successful?**

A Not especially, no more than anyone else
B Yes—because I work hard for it
C Yes—like everyone else, I find it easier to be at my best when I am happy and fulfilled

Final Scores

	A	B	C
Before			
After			

Analysis
Mostly As

These answers suggest you feel that the locus of control is outside of you, and that whatever you try will probably not succeed. Whatever you would like to happen in your future, it is likely to remain a daydream unless you take some action. To change things, follow the steps in the book and do the exercises (don't just read them). Starting with small, achievable steps, build up some reference experiences of successful goal attainment.

Mostly Bs

You are highly motivated, a bit of a perfectionist, and your own harshest critic. You don't like to be beaten and will force yourself to overcome challenges against the odds. You may find, however, that achieving your goals sometimes turns out to be less satisfying than you envisaged. Give some attention to clarifying what is important to you, and make sure you take account of how your goals impact on your health, relationships, and general happiness.

Mostly Cs

You demonstrate a mature approach to goal achievement—you take responsibility for your own actions, you are clear about what you want, and you think about the effects on your life and relationships. Make sure you do not become over-analytical about your goals, as this can lead to a lack of motivation. To recharge your drive, take care to stay connected with what is important to you, and try out new experiences from time to time.

Conclusion

If this is the first time you have done this self-assessment, then bear in mind this analysis as you read the book. Pay special attention to the areas highlighted by your responses, as well as the tips and techniques— these will help you to reduce the number of A responses next time around and achieve a more balanced mixture of B's and C's. After you have completed the book and put the techniques into practice, retake the assessment. Giving honest answers will enable you to get a direct measure of your progress—and you should see a big improvement!

It's Up to You

To reach your destination, you need to know where you are starting from. You can get clues about where you want to be from your life now, and how you arrived at this point. Your beliefs are self-fulfilling prophecies, so focusing on what you want and what is already working helps you reach your remaining goals. This section shows you:

- Why it's vital to take responsibility for where you are now
- How to use the Cause and Effect equation
- How to develop your personal power
- The power of your unconscious mind to help you to achieve what you want
- How to develop your self-awareness and assess where your life is now.

Take Responsibility

The first step in changing your life is to accept responsibility for where you are now. Recognize that you are the only person who can change your life— no one else can do it for you.

Make the Right Choices

To take responsibility is simply to recognize that you have the ability to respond to events as they happen. You cannot control what life throws at you. What you can control is the choices you make in response. This also means that you have a responsibility to make the best choices you can, and to keep learning so that you expand the range of choices available to you. The more abilities you have, the easier it is to make the right choice in any given situation. Does that mean you have to do it all yourself, without any outside assistance? No—there are some goals you can only achieve through working with others. You can't make other people help you—but you can influence and inspire them to want to help you in achieving your goals.

> To get results, action is necessary, as well as good intentions

Don't Self-blame

Taking responsibility is not the same as blaming yourself, or other people, for anything that has gone wrong up to now. Everyone (including you) makes the best choices they can according to how they perceive the world at the time. It makes no sense to feel guilty about things you have done in the past, because at that time you were doing the best that you could.

Happiness depends upon ourselves.

Aristotle

Think Feedback, not Failure

When you don't immediately get the result you wanted, you have a choice about how you view that result. One way of looking at things is likely to bring us more bad results; the other, however, gives us a chance to learn from mistakes so we don't repeat them. We can judge results we don't like either as "failure" or as "feedback"—information that allows us to correct our course. Which one will you choose?

Learn to Judge Your Results

If you become accustomed to thinking of yourself as a failure, you are setting up a vicious circle that can be hard to break. If, however, you take all your results—positive or negative—as feedback, you are setting up a progressive chain of events: one you can learn from.

Break the Circle of Failure

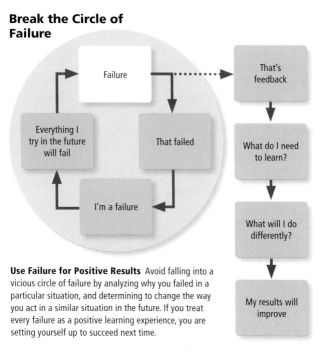

Use Failure for Positive Results Avoid falling into a vicious circle of failure by analyzing why you failed in a particular situation, and determining to change the way you act in a similar situation in the future. If you treat every failure as a positive learning experience, you are setting yourself up to succeed next time.

Make Your Good Fortune

Do you feel as though you are at the mercy of events, and that your chances for success are determined by your past history, your circumstances, and what other people will allow you to do? Or do you believe that you are the author of your own destiny, that you make your own luck, and that you can make a difference in your life? Most of us would put ourselves somewhere in between. The more you feel yourself sympathizing with the second viewpoint, the more likely you are to achieve your goals.

Cause and Effect

Many people put themselves at the Effect end of the spectrum. They feel that their emotions just happen to them, or are caused by other people. You can hear clues to the way people think in the words they choose to express themselves:

- She upset me
- He made me angry
- This gridlocked traffic is really getting to me!

By thinking this way, they are handing power over how they feel to other people—or even to inanimate objects—rather than taking charge of their feelings and using them to positive effect. They are saying that how they feel, and even what they do, is beyond their control. Is this how you want to be? Put yourself at Cause instead.

Change Your Position

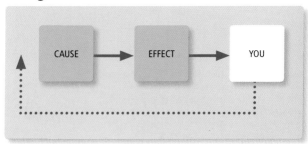

Identify Cause and Effect

CAUSE	EFFECT
Asks "How/What?"	Asks "Why?"
Has a present/future focus	Has a focus on the past
Learns from problems	Feels bad about problems

Focus on the Present

When you decide to place yourself at the Cause end of the spectrum, things change. You are more likely to believe in the principle that any problem can be solved, and you focus more on what you want than on what you don't. When problems arise, rather than asking "Why is this happening to me?" (a question focusing attention on the past), you ask things like:

- Exactly what is going on here?
- What can I do to change it?
- What is it that I want to happen instead?

These questions place your attention on the present and the future—a more useful focus than the past if you want to change.

Take Decisive Action Life often calls on you to act decisively. A medical team, for example, must constantly make key decisions on patient care.

Develop Your Personal Power

Your personal power is your ability to make choices for yourself. When the power is strong, life becomes much easier. You have the definite sense that you are in charge, and that the choices are yours to make.

Enjoy the Benefit

With a healthily developed sense of personal power, you will find you can manage your emotions, so you don't do things in the heat of the moment that you later regret. You do things because you want to, not just to please other people. You act more compassionately, because you are not feeling sorry for yourself. Your mind is calm and clear, yet alert. Whatever challenges you face, you are able to respond appropriately. Other people are attracted to you because you are comfortable with yourself.

Use Your Power to Act

Some people find themselves uncomfortable with the idea of "personal power," because for them it has connotations of dominance over other people, of ordering them around and telling them what to do. This is, however, a misconception of what is meant by the term. Personal power is about increasing your inner, personal strength— your reliance on yourself, and your ability to achieve your goals. You will find that as you build up reference experiences of achieving your goals, starting small at first and gradually increasing your level of challenge as you gain confidence, your "self-efficacy" (as psychologists call your sense of personal power) will grow, too. Once you have it, it is up to you to use that power wisely. If you are the sort of person who tends to feel martyred or put upon by other people, you will find that feeling gradually diminishing, and your sense of effectiveness growing, as you start to increase your personal power.

Affirm the positive, visualize the positive, and expect the positive.

Remez Sasson

Becoming Calm

This is a way of calming your mind and body fast. When stressful situations are sprung on you, you don't usually have time to do half an hour of yoga. You can use this exercise any time, anywhere.

→ Place your attention on a point straight in front of you and slightly above your eye level. Look at it with "soft eyes," without straining to focus, and blink whenever you want.

As the eyes relax, muscle tension leaves the body

→ Still looking straight ahead, allow your field of vision to gradually broaden out as you notice more and more of what is on either side of that point—until you are paying attention to what you can see out of the corners of your eyes on both sides at once.

→ Now let your awareness spread out even farther. Use your senses of hearing and spatial awareness to get a feeling of what is behind you as well.

→ Relax into this all-around awareness and notice what happens. Stay there for as long as you can.

What did you notice? Most people report a feeling of increasing relaxation—they notice that their breathing has slowed down, and that any internal dialogue or debate playing in their head has slowed down or even stopped altogether. Using your peripheral vision as an aid to calm like this need not be an intensive exercise. If you are giving a presentation, for example, going a little way into peripheral vision will help to calm any nervous butterflies you have, and will also enable you to see nonverbal responses across the whole audience, rather than concentrating too hard on individuals at the cost of an overview. To rest your eyes and return refreshed after the peripheral vision exercise, rub your hands together vigorously to warm them, and then place your palms over your closed eyes for a few seconds.

Center Yourself

Another way of increasing your personal power was inspired originally by the martial arts. It's a way of increasing your "presence," as well as a way of staying calm and centered no matter what happens around you. Martial arts practitioners discovered long ago that where you focus your attention in your body has a huge effect on how calm you are, how comfortable you are within yourself, and even how physically strong you are. Most practitioners attribute great power to this ability; some go so far as to say that when you are truly centered, it is impossible to feel fear—though this takes a lot of practice.

Increase Your Awareness

While you are out walking, practice paying attention to your central point and maintaining your peripheral vision. Although it might not be what you expect, as you focus on your central point, you will find that you also become considerably more aware of your surroundings. Many self-defense courses teach the development of this all-around awareness as a means of increasing your personal safety.

TECHNIQUES *to* practice

Use this exercise to locate your "center" and concentrate on your focus. It can be practiced in any quiet place where you can concentrate.

1 Stand with your feet shoulder-width apart, with your weight evenly balanced and your body relaxed.

2 Let your knees bend slightly, and concentrate your focus on the connection between your feet and the floor.

3 Pay attention to a point that is an inch or two below your navel, and in the center of your body, halfway between front and back. Locate the point mentally and focus on it completely.

4 Look straight ahead and go into peripheral vision.

Test How Centered You Are

It is easy both to test how centered you are, and to center yourself more strongly. Ask a friend to push your chest to try to make you take a step backward. Try this twice, the first time focusing on the top of your left ear, and the second time centered. You'll notice a dramatic difference.

Strength You may feel that whether or not someone can push you off balance is solely a question of physical strength. Change your focus, and you will find this is not the case.

Focus When you concentrate your energy in a peripheral part of your body (your left ear), you will find that you are easy to push off balance, even if you are trying hard to stay upright.

Center Once you have concentrated your energies centrally in your body, you will find that you are harder to push backward—even if you are consciously resisting the push less hard.

TIP Imagine projecting an "energy bubble" from your central point. Notice the results you get.

Clear Your Inner Clutter

If you feel as though there are too many things happening at once, and you don't know where to start, this is a sign that you need to clear some mental space. Otherwise you could end up constantly firefighting.

Be Effective, not Busy

Many people today believe that they "can't relax." Usually this is because they feel there is something that they don't want to face up to, so they try to distract themselves by keeping ceaselessly busy. The problem is that it doesn't work. On top of the time wasted on nonessential tasks (and you will already have discovered that any bit of trivia will do if your main purpose is just to stay busy), what they are trying to escape from doesn't go away. It is still nagging away at the back of the mind, distracting them from the very tasks they are using to distract themselves. When you face up to things, however, you will find that they will always be easier to deal with than you feared.

TECHNIQUES *to practice*

It helps to clear your mind completely before you make a start on something new. This is an easy mind-clearing exercise that can be practiced wherever you happen to be.

1 Close your eyes and focus on your breathing. You will find that in a short time it shifts into a more relaxed pattern.

2 If you hear any "mental chatter," let it happen. Left to itself, it will calm down.

3 As you stay focused on your breathing, you will find you notice certain sensations more than usual. Notice how the air you breathe in is cooler than the air you breathe out.

4 Each time you breathe in, let your attention follow each in-breath deeper down inside.

5 When you are ready to come back, open your eyes. Take a moment or two to notice how refreshed you feel.

Build an Inner Sanctuary

Where is your favorite place to relax? Everyone needs somewhere they can go to recharge their batteries and recover from the energy drains of modern life.

This exercise is designed to help you recharge your energies even when you're far away from a relaxing environment.

→ Find a comfortable place where you can close your eyes. Relax, using the breathing technique on the opposite page.

→ In your mind's eye, find your favorite place to relax. It could be a room in your house, somewhere that you've been on vacation, a memory from long ago, or even an imaginary place. This is somewhere just for you, where you can recharge.

→ Notice what you can see and be aware of the colors.

→ Listen to the peaceful, relaxing sounds.

→ Notice how peaceful it feels, as you begin to absorb the peace and tranquillity within yourself.

→ Stay for as long as feels right, then return refreshed.

Find Tranquillity When you have found your ideal internal refuge, you can take the time to perfect it until it meets all your criteria for recharging your energies.

The Power of Your Unconscious

The old-fashioned Freudian idea of the unconscious (sometimes called the subconscious) mind was of a kind of dungeon where we lock up all the repressed desires (aggression, lust, selfishness) that we can't admit to.

Recognize Your Unconscious

In fact, your unconscious mind is just those parts of your thought processes that happen below the radar of your conscious awareness. When you are talking to someone, who chooses the words and the order in which they come out? When you pick up your phone from the table, who is coordinating the dozens of muscles involved in that movement? What keeps you breathing when you are asleep? Not your conscious mind. Your unconscious mind is able to multitask in a way that is far beyond your conscious abilities.

Your unconscious mind is working in your favor

It keeps the billions of cells and thousands of systems in your body working in (more or less) perfect harmony. It runs your immune system, your digestive system, your breathing, your circulation, and it performs prodigious feats of real-time processing that the most advanced computers are nowhere near matching.

Learn to Use Your Unconscious

Your unconscious mind is like a faithful servant, carrying out your wishes without the need for conscious effort on your part. It wants you to succeed and it tries to act in your best interests. It likes to be given tasks to carry out. If you don't give it any instructions, it will take them from outside influences—usually drawing from advertising, the media, or peer pressure. Right now you can choose to enlist the help of your unconscious mind by being clear about what you want and giving it unambiguous instructions to follow.

Manage Your Mind

Your conscious mind (the "you" that makes decisions, or your "will") is like the captain of a ship. The unconscious mind plays the part of the crew. The crew members all know what their jobs are, and they can carry them out without having to be told. So what is the job of the captain? To decide where the ship is going. Many people, though, don't use their conscious mind for its intended purpose. On their "ship," the captain is forever worrying about whether the crew are doing their jobs, while neglecting to set a course for the ship. For long stretches they are becalmed, or going around in circles. Instead, you can select consciously the course you intend and let your unconscious mind get on with the job.

think SMART !

Your unconscious mind does not understand the word "not," so it's important that you learn to talk to your unconscious in a way that it will understand.

Get more effective results, both from your unconscious and from other people, by telling them what you do want them to do, rather than what you don't. If a parent tells a toddler "Don't touch that candy," the toddler's unconscious mind hears "touch that candy." Similarly, suppose that you want to give up smoking—if you constantly tell yourself "I'm not going to smoke," you will be continually reminding yourself of cigarettes, and probably restimulating your craving. Negation is a logical concept but you can't form an image of it, so focus your unconscious on positive benefits.

Work with Your Unconscious

Many people try to make changes through willpower alone, without first getting the agreement of the unconscious mind, or even considering what it might be trying to tell them. This behavior will make change feel like a chore, and it will usually fail; as soon as the person's conscious attention is elsewhere, the unconscious mind will go straight back to its old habits. Some self-help gurus treat the unconscious mind as a lazy servant, to be punished if it gets out of line. But what if those suppressed doubts turn out to be genuine concerns that were consciously overlooked? Far better to discover what you really want, at both the conscious and the unconscious levels of your mind, so you can get behind your goals in every possible way, and pursue them singlemindedly. That is what the processes in this book are designed to do.

5 minute FIX

If you need to make a quick decision, be sure you are happy with the answers to these questions before you act:

- Do I really want to make this change?
- If I make this change, what will I miss?
- What is the purpose of the behavior I am trying to change?
- What would be different if I made this change?

Recognize Your Feelings

Your unconscious mind uses your feelings to communicate with you. If you have ever made a big decision despite having some unfocused misgivings, because, rationally, you couldn't find a reason not to go ahead, you may have wished later that you had paid more attention to that small doubt, however quietly it was expressing itself. If you don't feel enthusiastic about a course of action but don't know why, it may be a sign that your conscious mind has missed something.

Use Sense and Instinct

A decision made based on your gut feeling only, though, could turn out as badly as one that

Common Instances of Self-sabotage

SELF-SABOTAGING BEHAVIOR	RESULTS
Trying to stop smoking when part of you doesn't want to	Relapsing early, failing in your attempt
Trying to lose weight without addressing the underlying issues	Repeating unsuccessful yo-yo dieting
Trying to be a success in a career you don't really like	Performing poorly; under-achieving at work
Wearing a business suit, but with sloppy grooming and accessories	People don't take you seriously

ignores your instincts. The ideal decisions are those in which you are conscious of an even balance between emotion and reason: a good decision will usually feel instinctively right and also make rational sense. When any major decision needs to be made, ask yourself if your proposed action meets both of these criteria. If it does, then you should act on it with confidence.

Inner Confidence The ultimate confidence derives from the certainty that a decision is right for you on both rational and emotional levels.

Use Your Beliefs Positively

The beliefs you choose become filters through which you interpret everything that happens. Evidence that supports your chosen beliefs will be highlighted, while evidence that contradicts them will be played down or not even noticed. Here are two beliefs you may have come across:

"Life's a bitch and then you die."

"Life is an adventure, people are basically good, and I can achieve anything I want."

Which one is true? If you think about it, you can provide evidence from your own life to support either one. So both—or neither—are true. Beliefs are like maps that help us find our way around. The important question about them is not "Are they true?" but "Are they useful?" Which belief you choose becomes a filter through which you interpret everything that happens. Evidence that supports your chosen belief will be highlighted, while evidence that contradicts it will be ignored, played down, or even go unnoticed.

Read the Appropriate Map Maps come in different guises—think about a weather map against a road map: both of them are accurate, but which is the more useful for your purposes?

Consider the Evidence

The "life's a bitch" believer will act in a way that makes sense to them in the light of that belief, which will be very different from how someone holding the second belief acts. The results they get—positive or negative—will tend to bear out their belief. The longer and more deeply held the belief is, the more "evidence" it will accumulate in support of it. There are many well-known examples of research studies supporting the idea that what you believe influences the real outcome of events in your life.

Your beliefs are the script for your life

Three effects that are often cited are:

- The "Placebo Effect," in which some patients in the "control group" in clinical drug trials get better, convinced that they are receiving medicine, even though the "treatment" that they think they are receiving is just a sugar pill

- The "Halo Effect," discovered by Edward Thorndike in 1920—this established that if you strongly favor one particular and specific characteristic that you find in a person, you are more likely to rate the same person higher for a variety of other positive traits, whether or not you have evidence to support your rating.

- The "Pygmalion Effect," described by Robert Rosenthal in 1968—which showed that how effectively and successfully children perform academically is strongly influenced by their teachers' beliefs in their skills.

Since what you believe tends to become true for you, it's important to think carefully about what you believe to make sure that it supports your success.

TIP **Make a positive effort to look for evidence that disproves and disempowers any beliefs that are working to limit you.**

Focus on What You Want

Human beings are born with the ability to see patterns in things. Where there are no innate patterns, we tend to project them—like seeing pictures in a campfire, or faces and animals in clouds.

Learn to Look

Consequently, it is much easier to notice something if we are already expecting to see it. The implication of this for changing your life is that you get what you focus on. If you focus on what you want, you will find it; if all you focus on is getting away from what you don't want, that is what you will find yourself returning to again and again.

Choose the Right Motivation

There are two kinds of motivation—toward what you want, and away from what you don't want. While "away from" motivation can be useful in administering the kick that you needed to get started, it will give you inconsistent results. To help you keep going until you reach your goals, you need to ensure that your motivation is mainly focused on "toward."

Identify Your Motivation

"TOWARD" MOTIVATION	"AWAY-FROM" MOTIVATION
Has built-in direction: you know where you are going, and can make corrections if necessary.	Lacks direction: when you want to get away from something, any direction will do.
Works in a sustained way: you will find that it exerts an even stronger pull as you come closer to your goal, and will help to inspire you.	Works only for a short time: it gives out as soon as you get far enough away from what you are avoiding, leaving you becalmed until the next threat comes along.
Inspires you: even if your current situation is unpleasant, your mental image is of where you want to be.	Proves to be stressful: the mental image that motivates you is of what you want to get away from.

Get Results Every Time

One of the chief arguments against "away from" motivation is that it leads to inconsistent results. If someone is motivated to make money primarily because she grew up in poverty and never wants to go back there, her motivation will begin to disappear as she starts getting rich, and return once she has lost her money. Behavioral experts have surmised that this is the reason that some millionaires make and lose their fortunes several times over—they are working to "away from" motivation.

Motivation

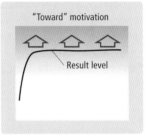

Pick Your Motivation Reach your goal with "toward" motivation. "Away from" motivation only helps you escape from what you don't want.

Limit the Drama in Your Life

We all face a certain amount of challenge and difficulty, some far more than others. However, some people seem to attract difficulties even in quite straightforward situations where none previously existed. This may reflect an unconscious need to be the hero or heroine in their own life story. When things are going well, they will unconsciously find a way of disrupting them so that they can continue in their heroic struggle.

TIP **Ask yourself if you would be happy to get what you want easily. You may be creating more drama than you need to be successful.**

Look at Your Life Appreciatively

Social psychologists have discovered that positive emotions give us benefits beyond just feeling good. When you feel good, it's easier to see the big picture, rather than getting lost in detail.

Foster Creativity

When you experience positive emotions, you are more creative than when you are feeling "neutral." Positive emotions help you to make sense of complex information quickly, and make you less likely to jump to conclusions. A positive mindset has physical benefits, too—it helps heart rate and blood pressure to return to normal more quickly after stressful events.

> **Every experience, positive or negative, can be used to learn**

Cultivate an Appreciative Mindset

Because positive emotions have these benefits, it is useful to build on what is positive in your life as a basis for making the changes you want. However, it is not always easy to try to stimulate positive emotions through humor, or through telling ourselves to look on the bright side. Researchers in the rapidly growing field of "positive psychology" tell us that the easiest positive emotions to evoke, even under extreme circumstances, are those of gratitude and compassion. You can use this to:

- Appreciate even simple things with gratitude.
- When bad things happen, ask yourself, "What do I need to learn from this?"
- Find positive meaning through helping—act compassionately toward others.

It is of practical value to learn to like yourself.

Norman Peale

Make the Most of Good Memories

Your emotional response to a mental image is determined at least as much by the way in which you think about it as by what it is that you are thinking about.

The visual qualities of an image tell the brain how much attention to pay. Your response is stronger when an image is vivid, and when you are involved in it. Try this experiment:

→ Think of a happy memory. As you see it in your mind's eye, notice how intense your positive emotional response is.
→ Is the picture life-size, or smaller? Bring it up to life-size.
→ Is it in color, or black and white? Make it colorful.
→ Try making it a little brighter. Then put some movement into it.
→ Step into the picture and see it through your own eyes.

Notice what happens to the intensity of how the memory makes you feel after each of the steps above.

Use Past and Future Positive images, filled with texture and movement, are effective motivational aids, whether they derive from memories or future hopes.

Find What Is Already Working

There is an increasingly popular approach to organizational and personal change called Appreciative Inquiry, which holds that the best way to improve things is to discover what is already working and then do more of it. We tend to get more of what we focus on. Paying attention to what is already working well in your life is likely to raise your morale and your self-esteem, and increase the energy available for changing the areas of your life that are not working so well.

Know Your Strengths

To make it easier to establish the positives in your mind, try these lines of inquiry:

- What do people tell you are your strengths?
- What do the people who care about you regard as your

Accentuate the Positive

This exercise is designed to help you focus on the aspects of your life that you want to keep. Even if you have been telling yourself that your life is terrible, there are always some positive elements.

→ Rate how positive you feel at right now on a scale of 1 to 10.

→ What is working in your life? Write it down—it doesn't matter how trivial each element seems. Go into as much detail as you can. Notice how you feel about each small element.

→ What are you proud of? Again, describe each event and notice what it means to you, and how you feel about it.

→ What are you good at?

→ Revisit how you feel, and rate it on the 1-to-10 scale again. To increase the positive effect, you can retrace the steps above, adding more detail, so that you really involve yourself with each positive image.

good qualities and abilities? Take a look at yourself through their eyes or, better still, ask them—you may be pleasantly surprised.

- Imagine that a good friend was talking about you to someone who has not met you. How would that friend describe your good points?

Building on what is already strong makes it stronger

Notice how you feel after focusing on the positive aspects of your life. What has changed?

Learn to Value Acceptance

Until you are in a position to change the parts of your life that you do not like, the best attitude to have is one of acceptance. There is no point wasting your energy fretting about things you are not in a position to change. One of the best-known expressions of the attitude of acceptance is the "Serenity Prayer," usually attributed to the theologian Reinhold Niebuhr. It shows a wisdom that resonates beyond any particular religious tradition:

God grant me the serenity
to accept the things I cannot change;
courage to change the things I can;
and the wisdom to know the difference.

Do More of What Works

In contrast to problem-focused approaches to change, the Appreciative Inquiry approach says that you will get more sustainable changes if you concentrate on doing more of what is working in your life. It is easier to envisage the future you want when it is based on your own experiences, rather than trying to dream it up in its entirety.

TIP Make sure your vision of the future keeps the good aspects of your life now: this will reduce your resistance to change.

Summary: Think Positively

A negative approach to life or lack of self-confidence does more than just make you feel bad about yourself. It can also stop you from taking the positive steps you need in order to reach your goals. To get where you want to go, you must learn to take responsibility for your life, approach it with confidence, and make the most of the opportunities you find.

Plan of Action

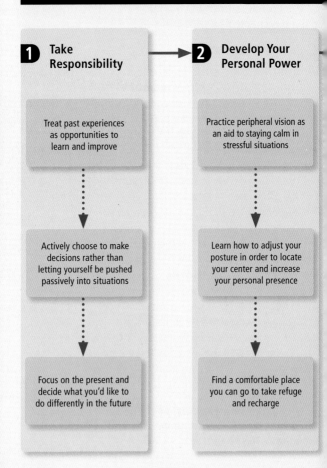

1 Take Responsibility

Treat past experiences as opportunities to learn and improve

↓

Actively choose to make decisions rather than letting yourself be pushed passively into situations

↓

Focus on the present and decide what you'd like to do differently in the future

2 Develop Your Personal Power

Practice peripheral vision as an aid to staying calm in stressful situations

↓

Learn how to adjust your posture in order to locate your center and increase your personal presence

↓

Find a comfortable place you can go to take refuge and recharge

3 **Enlist Your Unconscious** → **4** **Look at Your Life Appreciatively**

Recognize where your feelings and instincts want to take you

Pay attention to what is working well in your life and identify your strengths

⋮

⋮

Identify what motivates you and use this to give yourself focus

Accept and make the most of those things that you cannot change

⋮

⋮

Focus on moving toward what you want, rather than trying to run away from things that you don't want

Concentrate on doing more of those things that work well in your life

Develop Your Self-Awareness

The more conscious you are of the ways in which you think and behave, the easier you will find it to identify elements that call for change. Developing your self-awareness is a powerful aid to achieving your goals.

Listen to What You Say

"It's a jungle out there"; "I've put that behind me." These are metaphors, a common way to express things. When someone says "I'm in a bad relationship," they are talking as if the relationship is some kind of container. If they were speaking literally, they would say something like "I am relating badly to this other person." The implications of the metaphor—that the relationship has some kind of existence of its own outside of the speaker—are different from those of the second statement. In the first case, it's as if there's nothing the person can do about the relationship; in the second case, the speaker can decide to make changes in the way they are relating.

5 minute FIX

To make sense of an unfamiliar situation fast, find a positive metaphor for it before you act.

This gives you the right mental attitude to find a way through to a solution.

- Think of wide open metaphors —a door opening, a broad sweep of landscape—rather than small, enclosed ones.

- When you can think what something unfamiliar is like, you feel comfortable with it.

- Then come back to the situation and calmly think it through.

Express Yourself

Our emotional state from moment to moment is a response not just to external events but to our internal world—the memories that fleetingly come to mind and our images of what might happen in the future. The metaphors you use will subtly affect how you feel, and any metaphors that you use habitually will shape both the way you think and

think
SMART

if you feel your life is in a rut, and you cannot find a way to progress, use metaphor to help you think creatively. Find a metaphor for where you are right now, and develop it to see how you might move on.

A journey is a universal metaphor for life that anyone can relate to: goals are destinations, challenges are obstacles along the way, and so on. You could ask yourself, if your life were like a journey, what kind of journey would it be? You can write your answer or discuss it with someone else. The answers can be very revealing. A life that is like a train journey that does not stop at the right station, for example, may reveal that you need to pay more attention, and to take more control of your direction.

your mood. What images do your habitual metaphors evoke? Do you work with someone who is "a pain"? Is your family life "a nightmare"? Or is everything "running smoothly"? If you use unpleasant images, you are evoking matching emotions in your listeners—including yourself.

Recognize Your "Self"

One of the most common yet least recognized metaphors is the "self." We talk about the self as if it is a lazy servant ("I'm finding it hard to motivate myself") or an unruly child ("I have no self-discipline"). This distances you from the fact that there is just the one person there—you. Remember that whatever you do, or don't do, is your choice and your responsibility.

TIP **If you find yourself using negative metaphors, ask yourself, "What else is this situation like? How else could I describe it?"**

Chart Your Personal Highs and Lows

HIGH IMPACT
- Winning a diploma
- Earning a degree in a subject I loved, but found challenging
- Finally getting the right marketing job
- The births of my children
- My promotion last year

NEGATIVE IMPACT
- Failing my driving test
- Spending two years in a job I disliked
- Being passed over for the position in New York
- My divorce
- My poor record in sales

Chart the Highs and Lows of Your Life

Another way of viewing your life is to list high and low points (a brief example is shown above). When you have completed your list, look back over it. Notice how each significant experience in your life has helped to make you the person you are today. First, take credit for making the high points happen. Ask yourself these questions:
- How did I contribute to that being a high point?
- What was I doing right?

Learn from the Low Points

Remember that there is something positive to learn from the worst experiences, even if it is only how to prevent a similar experience from happening again. Facing adversity develops your character—if you choose to learn from it. Ask yourself these questions:
- What positive things have I learned from that experience?
- In what ways has this made me a stronger/wiser/more compassionate person?

Imagine that your life is being made into a movie. Which episodes would the director emphasize to make an inspiring story? Which episodes would be selected if it was a feel-good comedy?

Keep a Journal

As well as reviewing your life with the benefit of hindsight, you can learn from as it unfolds by reflecting on it each day. Writing your thoughts down helps you detach yourself from them, as well as teaching you more about yourself.

Re-reading past entries, even comparatively recent ones written just a month or two ago, will show you how much your emotional state influences how you think and what you write.

→ Ten minutes of writing a day is enough to give you useful results; it becomes effortless once you get into the habit.

→ Write whatever you think, without analyzing it or pre-planning what you are going to say.

→ Find the time of day that works best for you. First thing in the morning (before your mind gets involved in the day's distractions), when you come home from work (to draw a line between work and leisure), and last thing at night are all popular choices, according to taste.

Tuesday, April 24

A wonderful sunrise this morning made it feel particularly inspiring to be up so early and have time to focus on the day ahead.

The office was tense with the reorganization in full swing, but the new manager seems reasonable and is turning out to be good at compromise in tricky situations.

Planning for the trip to the New York office is going smoothly, and I've been given the job of overseeing the schedule for the delegates. I'm trying not to get too nervous about it, since I know that I don't perform at my best when I'm tense.

Decide 2 What's Important

To harness the positive power of "toward" motivation, you need to be clear about what you want. When you are busy dealing with the ever-increasing demands of everyday life, it is easy to get distracted from giving your own needs and wishes the attention they deserve. This section is about focusing on what is really important to you. It shows you:

- How to distinguish between "urgent" and "important"
- How to clarify your values
- How to check for and resolve inner conflicts and potential self-sabotage

Look Ahead

Do you live for the moment, or is your life planned out in detail from now until beyond retirement? Probably you fall somewhere between the two. You need to look at how to make a vision of the future work for you.

Where Is Your Time Horizon?

If you own a business, the discipline of having to create a business plan may already have forced you to make plans beyond your natural time horizon. In our personal lives, most of us could benefit from giving some sustained attention to the longer term. Looking farther ahead allows you to sidestep some of the nasty surprises that life can throw at you, and means that you spend less time in "firefighting" mode trying to deal with unexpected events.

Work toward Your Goals

If it is not easy to think of your goals for six years ahead, this is valuable information in itself. Treat it as a sign that it is worth spending some time deciding what you want in the future. Remember that this is just a starting point. You can add to your goals as more ideas come to you. You may find that you get clearer about your vision for the future as you complete the exercises in the next few pages. They will help you clarify your values. Don't be surprised if your goals change altogether, or radically expand, as you raise your sights and discover more about what you want.

Long- versus Short-term Views

HIGH IMPACT	NEGATIVE IMPACT
Taking a long-term view	Taking a short-term view
• Enables proactive decisions	• Ensures reactive behavior
• Works with "toward" motivation	• Works with "away from" motivation
• Is driven by possibility	• Is driven by necessity
• Offers choice	• Compels you to act

To encourage yourself to focus beyond your everyday concerns, however pressing, take ten minutes to ask yourself these questions and write down your answers. They will help you to gain a broad overview of your situation.

1 What are your goals for six years from now?

2 What are your goals for three years from now?

3 What are your goals for one year from now?

It is best to start with your six-year goals, because the medium-term and shorter-term goals will often be stepping stones on the way to your long-term destination.

Place Important over Urgent

Stephen Covey, the well-known author on business and time management, draws a distinction between tasks that demand to be done immediately, and tasks that are important. He points out that the important tasks often get pushed to the back of the line, because we are too busy dealing with the urgent ones—even those that are not important. The important tasks often only get done in a mad scramble, when they become urgent because a deadline is looming. The key is to know what is important, and to stay focused on it. Once you have some meaningful long-term goals to work toward, the steps that will get you there become important, and it is easier to prioritize your time. Tackling the important tasks first will increase your sense of control over your workload, reduce your stress levels and—most important of all—ensure that you accomplish much more.

TIP Ask yourself, "What am I putting off right now?"—and do it immediately, without conducting any more internal will I?/won't I? debates.

Know Your Values

Your values give you motivation for your actions. Follow the numbered stages in this section to establish which values are important to you, and ensure that you are clear about what you are working toward.

Your Personal Scale of Values

Your values are also your criteria for judging if something is right or wrong. They guide your decisions and give meaning to your life. This guidance operates at a more or less unconscious level; you don't need to think about it. Once you become aware of your values, you can use them as a checklist to evaluate any choices you are offered.

Find Your Values

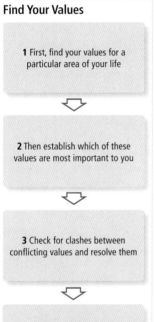

1 First, find your values for a particular area of your life

2 Then establish which of these values are most important to you

3 Check for clashes between conflicting values and resolve them

4 Check for "away from" motivation in the final set of values

How Values Originate

You acquire your values as you grow up, from a variety of influences around you—they might include your parents, your peers, or the popular culture of your childhood and youth. Over time, in adulthood, you will also find that you modify your values in the light of the conclusions you draw for yourself from the events of your life. Values are abstract concepts (like *fun*, *integrity*, *learning*, or *security*), so you can satisfy them in many different ways. Use the four numbered stages shown in outline on the left, and expanded on the following pages, to identify and organize your values.

Get the Best from the Process

Eliciting your values is a simple yet powerful process—use these tips to make it more revealing. It may be easier for someone else to ask you the questions, instead of asking them of yourself:

→ Values should be abstract. If you reach a "concrete" answer (like "a good company car" as a career value), ask again "What's important about that?" until you reach an abstract.

→ Even when you think you have run out of answers, asking "What's important about <area>?" will often unearth important values that you were less consciously aware of.

→ The more honest you are with yourself, the more valuable your list will be to you.

→ If your values list includes a word like "satisfaction," "fulfillment," or "contentment," check what that word means to you. If it is what you would get if all the other values on the list were present, you can safely take it out.

1 Find Your Values for a Specific Area

The first step is to think of the area of your life that you want to change first. When you have decided what it is, ask yourself the following questions:

• What is important to me about <area>?

Write down the immediate answer that comes to mind. Then continue to ask:

• What else is important to me about <area>?

You will probably end up with a list of around seven to ten points of importance relating to that area—although it may be less and it may be more. These points are the values that you hold for that area of your life. Keep a note of them, and revisit them if you need to.

> It's not hard to make decisions when you know what your values are.
>
> Roy Disney

2 Establish Your Most Important Values

Some values will be more important to you than others. The most important values will be the ones that have the most say in how you use your time, so the next step in clarifying your priorities for your chosen area will be to discover your values hierarchy. The first value that came to mind in the previous exercise may not be the most important. In fact, some of the "submerged" values that came at the end of the list may be the ones that turn out to be most important to you. Eliciting your values hierarchy is simple. Just take your list of values for a given area and ask yourself:

- If I could only have one of these values in <area>, which one would it have to be?'

When you have identified that value, ask:

- If I could only have one more, which one would it be?

and so on, until you have all the values in order.

Look at the example below, using values for "Work and Career."

Initial List		Revised priority order	
Enjoyment	4	1	Integrity
Learning	8	2	Making a difference
Security	5	3	Money
People	6	4	Enjoyment
Recognition	7	5	Security
Money	3	6	People
Respect	9	7	Recognition/ Respect
Making a difference	2	8	Learning
Integrity	1		

Deciding between Values

If it's hard to decide which is the more important of two values,
use this method:

→ You can have **either** one value or the other, but not both.
  Which does it have to be?
→ You may find that a value in your initial list turns out
  to be the same as, or a slightly different aspect of, another
  value. If this happens, merge them—so *respect* and
  recognition might become *respect/recognition*.
→ You can write the values on sticky notes to make it easier to
  reorder them—it also makes the process more physically
  interactive, so it may give you a deeper connection with it.

Money as a Value

If money comes out at the top of the list, you may need
to do some additional work on your list. Ideally, money
would be a "means" value, one that is useful because
having it helps to fulfill abstract "ends" values. For
example, having money might allow you to have more
security, or freedom. Money does not make a good "ends"
value. If someone has money at the top of their values list,
they could end up with a large amount of money, but find
that it means nothing to them.

Keep Your Priorities Flexible

The values that are most important to you may change
over time as your circumstances change. If someone is
heavily in debt, money may be high on their scale of
values. Once they have a comfortable amount in the bank,
money might be less important, and other values move up
the list. The values hierarchy that you elicited in Stage 2 is
a snapshot of where you are at this point in time.

3 Check for Clashes between Values

Conflicting values (for example, adventure versus security in your career) can make you feel torn between them. Here's how to check that your values are compatible:

- Take the lowest value on your prioritized list and check it against the one above it. Can you have both? If you feel that the two values cannot coexist, mark an X at the clash. Continue to check the lowest value against every other value, all the way up the list.
- Then take the next lowest value, and check it against each value above it in turn.
- Continue with the next lowest value until you have checked each value against all the values above it.

Read Your Chart

In the sample chart below, the subject feels that "enjoyment" and "money," and "security" and "recognition" are in conflict with each other. They need to ask more questions to resolve how the clashing values can be met, or to decide on the more important of the two.

Potential Values Clashes

	Integrity	Making a difference	Money	Enjoyment	Security	People	Recognition
Integrity	✓	✓	✓	✓	✓	✓	✓
Making a difference	✓	✓	✓	✓	✓	✓	✓
Money	✓	✓	✓	✗	✓	✓	✓
Enjoyment	✓	✓	✗	✓	✓	✓	✓
Security	✓	✓	✓	✓	✓	✓	✓
People	✓	✓	✓	✓	✓	✓	✓
Recognition	✓	✓	✓	✓	✓	✓	✓
Learning	✓	✓	✓	✓	✓	✓	✓

What Your Answers Say about Motivation

YOUR ANSWER	WHAT TYPE OF MOTIVATION?
"Because I've been poor, and I didn't like it."	"Away from" motivation
"Because of all the wonderful things I could do with it."	"Toward" motivation
"Well, you need money."	Concealed "away from" motivation— if you say you need something, what is really on your mind is what will happen if you don't have it.
"It's better to have money."	Another concealed "away from"— better than what? Than not having it.
"Because I can buy things, and I can use it to benefit people, and it provides a safety net."	Mostly "toward," with some "away from"

4 Check for "Away From" Motivation

Motivation can be toward what you want, away from what you don't want, or a mixture of the two. "Away from" motivation usually runs out before you reach your goal, so you may find that values that are mainly "away from" will not be fulfilled consistently. The key question for detecting the direction of motivation in each value is "**Why** is <value> important?" In the chart above, you can see a range of answers to the question "Why is money important?", alongside the motivation underpinning each one. Although "why?" is not a useful question to ask in a problem-solving situation (it tends to elicit either excuses or justifications), it is a valuable one when you are trying to establish motivation. To answer the question, you have to analyze the thinking underpinning your actions, and it will become clear what your motivation is.

***

TIP Become more aware of other people's motivation by noticing the "toward" and "away from" clues in what they say.

Resolve Values Conflicts

If you discovered that two of your values conflict with one another, there are several possible methods for you to try to work toward a resolution.

Satisfy Both Values

Ask yourself what needs to happen to make it possible to satisfy both values at the same time. Then make it happen. Alternatively, take one of the clashing values and ask yourself: "If I have that value fully, what would it give me that is even more important?" This should give you a higher value. Ask the same question until you can't get any higher. Then do the same thing with the other value. You may find that the higher values are more compatible with one another than the lower ones were.

Moving to "Toward"

Ask yourself some searching questions:

- If you are mainly focused on what you want to get away from or avoid, what do you want instead of that?
- If you knew that you were completely safe from what you want to avoid, and there was no chance of its happening, what would that free you up to do?
- If your practical and financial needs would be met whatever you did, what would you want to do?

CASE study: Reconciling the Options

Doing a good job and quality time with his family are both important to Yukio. He found, though, that staying late at work was eating into his family time and left him feeling resentful while at work, and anxious while at home: in neither place was he giving his best.

- *Yukio looked at his time management and made some efficiency savings, enabling him to get away from work earlier.*
- *Yukio learned to balance two conflicting requirements. As he felt less tense, his creativity at work actually improved.*

Give Your Values Voices

Use visualization to give your conflicting values their own voices. Step outside yourself and see how they negotiate with each other. By objectifying your values, you will find it easier to establish what is really important to you.

→ Imagine you have one of your values sitting in the palm of your hand. What does it look like? What does its voice sound like? Do the same with the other value, in the other hand.

→ Ask one of the values what it is trying to do for you and what is really important to it. Imagine an answer that feels right.

→ Repeat the process with the other value.

→ Ask the two values if they now realize that they both want the best for you.

→ Ask each value to tell the other what it needs to know.

→ Imagine what the two would look like if they merged.

→ When the values are as close as possible, let your hands relax as you take the values back. Take a little time and ways of fulfilling both may come to you.

Personalize Your Values As they acquire their own voices, you will find it much easier to act as an objective mediator between them.

Summary: Know Your Values

The values that are important to you, the abstract concepts such as love, friendship, security, or recognition, provide motivation for your actions and help guide your decisions. For any area of your life that you want to change, it is helpful to think about the values that inspire you in that area of your life—and the conflicts between these concepts.

Plan of Action

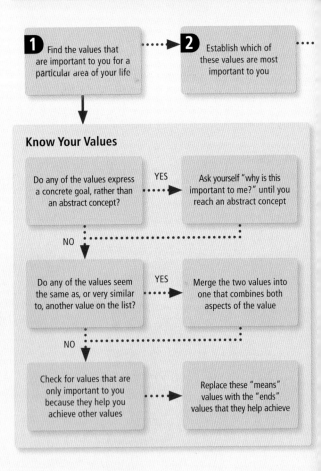

1 Find the values that are important to you for a particular area of your life

2 Establish which of these values are most important to you

Know Your Values

Do any of the values express a concrete goal, rather than an abstract concept?

YES Ask yourself "why is this important to me?" until you reach an abstract concept

NO

Do any of the values seem the same as, or very similar to, another value on the list?

YES Merge the two values into one that combines both aspects of the value

NO

Check for values that are only important to you because they help you achieve other values

Replace these "means" values with the "ends" values that they help achieve

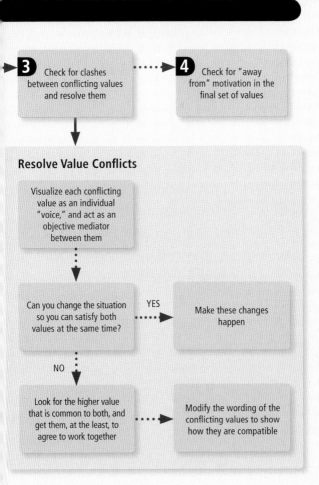

3 Check for clashes between conflicting values and resolve them

4 Check for "away from" motivation in the final set of values

Resolve Value Conflicts

Visualize each conflicting value as an individual "voice," and act as an objective mediator between them

↓

Can you change the situation so you can satisfy both values at the same time? —— **YES** ——▶ Make these changes happen

NO

↓

Look for the higher value that is common to both, and get them, at the least, to agree to work together —— ▶ Modify the wording of the conflicting values to show how they are compatible

Clear
the
Blocks

3

The biggest obstacles to achieving our goals are within ourselves. To set out for your goals with confidence that you will achieve them, you first need to let go of any limiting beliefs and clear out any blocks within yourself. This section will help you to:

• Identify and loosen up limiting beliefs
• Get yourself out of a rut
• Defuse the triggers for problems
• Handle your inner critic
• Deal with difficult people

Defeat Limiting Beliefs

Anything you believe that holds you back can be described as a limiting belief. It could be a belief about your own capabilities, about how the world works, or about how you or other people should behave.

Look at Your Beliefs

As a child, you take your beliefs from other people. Once you have some beliefs in place, you use them as the basis for forming new beliefs. As soon as you start basing your beliefs on other beliefs, rather than on the evidence of your senses, you lose the reality check that would make you update your beliefs in the light of new evidence. What you tell yourself acts like a self-hypnotic suggestion—it begins to influence your view of reality. This is all the more insidious because most of the time you are not consciously paying attention to your internal dialogue, so what it is saying goes unchallenged by your conscious mind.

Our longest-held beliefs may be the most limiting

Identify Limiting Beliefs

Becoming aware of beliefs that you find limiting is the first step to changing them. They are not always obvious, but they usually show up first at a conscious level as feelings of discomfort, irritation, or anxiety when thinking about a particular issue. For example, if you're worried about putting yourself forward for promotion at work, you could say out loud, "I can do that job easily." Your immediate inner response might be "No I couldn't, they'll see through me in a minute—I don't have enough experience," and so on. So you could write down the three limiting beliefs, exactly as you expressed them to yourself internally:

- I couldn't do that job
- They'll see through me
- I don't have enough experience

Check Your Self-Talk

INDICATOR WORD OR PHRASE	WHAT IT INDICATES AND WHAT TO ASK YOURSELF
Should, ought to	If you have rules for how people "should" behave, you are setting yourself up for disappointment when they don't live up to these standards. Ask yourself: "What would happen if I/they don't?"
I must, I have to	This way of thinking indicates that you feel compelled to do something, rather than willingly choosing to do it. But are you really compelled? To uncover what is behind this feeling, ask yourself: "What will happen if I don't?"
Makes me	As in "She makes me angry." This abdicates your personal responsibility by assuming that another person has control over your feelings or actions. Ask yourself: "Really? How did what she did or said cause me to get angry?"
I can't	If this means "I can't do this yet," ask: "What stops you?" If it means "I don't want to," ask: "What would happen if you did?"
Always, never, everyone, nobody	This indicates a sweeping generalization, to which there will usually be exceptions. Just put a question mark after the word "always?"
Try	"Try" indicates that you are doubtful, or that you may not succeed. Instead, say "I will."

Challenge Your Beliefs

Just writing the limiting beliefs down distances them from you and starts to loosen them up. Since you are now aware of them, you can begin to question if they are really true. Limiting beliefs are often indicated by recurring words and phrases in what we say. If you find yourself using any of these phrases in your internal dialogue, ask yourself the indicated question to uncover the limiting belief and reconnect it with reality. With practice, you will soon find that these phrases ring alarm bells for you and warn you if you are straying into negative thought patterns.

Loosen Limiting Beliefs

Even if you have held some of the beliefs that limit you for a very long time, you can still loosen them comparatively easily. Try the following techniques:

- Turn them into questions. Add a question mark onto the end of each belief and say it out loud as a question. This introduces doubt and makes you compare the belief with your current reality—a lot may have happened since you acquired the belief originally and it may no longer be true. If you are doubtful about your ability to do a job, for example, saying "I don't have enough experience?" automatically makes you start looking for examples of relevant experience from your work history up to now.

- Ask yourself where the belief came from. As children, we internalize things that people tell us. At an early age we can't use logic to check the validity of what we are told, so we just accept it. Think about when you first acquired that limiting belief—it may be older than you think—and who you got it from. Now that you have your adult wisdom and powers of logic, would you still choose to take that belief on board?

- Ask yourself what the belief is costing you. If you go on believing this, what will the negative effect be? If you choose to believe something more empowering, what will you gain?

think SMART

By reformulating the limiting belief as an aspirational question, you can turn it around.

If you put the words "How can I…" in front of the problematic belief, you turn it into a direction for action. For example, you can replace "I don't have the time" with "How can I find the time?"

Rehearsing New Beliefs

If simply installing a new set of beliefs seems too hard to you, try them out by mentally rehearsing how they will feel. It will help you realize that it is possible to change the way you think and act.

→ Identify what you would choose to believe instead of the limiting belief.
→ Run a mental movie in which you see yourself acting from the new belief, in a situation where it is appropriate.
→ Repeat the movie, making it more vivid each time, until it starts to look convincing.
→ Make any adjustments you need to.
→ Step into the "you" in the movie and run it again, so that you can feel what it is like to act from the new belief. Notice how things turn out differently.
→ Try out acting on your new belief in a non-threatening real-life situation and notice how things turn out differently.

• Ask yourself what the belief is trying to do for you. What is the positive intention behind that belief? (For example, it may be trying to preserve you from disappointment.) Is it achieving it? Try to think of ways in which you can let go of the belief but achieve the positive outcome it was trying to get for you.
• Ask yourself if everyone believes the same thing. Does everyone you know share this limiting belief? If you can think of someone who does not, what enables them to believe something different? If they can do it, then you should be able to, too.

TIP Look back over your life history for repeating patterns. When you learn from your mistakes, you don't have to repeat them.

Deal with Problems

Any problem has a three-part structure, which gives you three ways to tackle it: change the situation, change how you interpret it, or change your response to it. Even if the first is not possible, the other two always are.

Stay Relaxed and Positive

Sometimes your mind's attempts to solve a problem can actually help to keep the problem in place. For example, someone who has suffered a bad relationship breakup may find themselves pulling back emotionally when their new partner gets too serious. This could result in the breakup of the current relationship—the very thing they were trying to avoid. Trying to solve a problem by continually turning it over in your mind may embed it deeper. The "solution focus" approach in therapy suggests a different method: if you focus your attention on what life would be like if the problem were solved, you will be more likely to think and act in ways that leave the problem behind.

Focus on the Solution

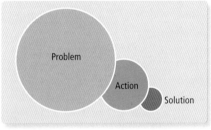

What is Important?
If you let the problem occupy all the foreground, you can hardly see the solution; reverse the scale, and the solution is clear

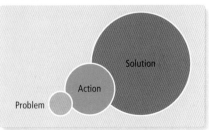

Getting Yourself Out of a Rut

Sometimes you can find yourself going over and over your problems, feeling low in energy, and telling yourself that there is nothing to look forward to. If you ever get into that kind of rut, here are some tried-and-tested ways to get yourself out of it.

Exercise: research shows that regular vigorous exercise produces brain chemicals that have the effect of making us feel good.

Plan things to look forward to: remember to schedule treats for yourself even when you are busy and distracted, to avoid "empty weekend" syndrome.

Interrupt recurring patterns: if you are getting stuck in a familiar pattern that is affecting your energy, interrupt it by doing something different. Get some ideas by asking yourself:

➔ What would my favorite TV character do instead?
➔ What is the most out-of-character thing I could do?
➔ What would a concerned friend advise me to do?

Use the Miracle Question

So whatever the problem you are trying to solve, ask yourself this question: "If a miracle were to happen tonight while I am asleep, so the problem was completely solved, what is going to tell me that the problem has gone away when I wake up tomorrow?" Think around the answer, giving it the time it deserves, and go into as much detail as possible on what the solution will seem like and how it will change things. A good supplementary back-up question to get you thinking about how you will be behaving differently is: "How will other people around me be able to tell that this miracle has happened?"

> **The universe is change; our life is what our thoughts make it.**
>
> Marcus Aurelius

Scale the Problem

Try this question: where would you place the problem you are dealing with on a scale of 1 to 10, where 1 is the worst it has ever been and 10 is where you will be when the problem is completely solved? Assigning the number activates the left hemisphere of the brain, which is more associated with positive emotions than the right. To move toward action, ask what would be different if you were one number above your current rating. How would your thoughts, feelings, actions, and the outside world differ? This will help you to take the first step toward a solution.

Use Your Thoughts to Help

Common sense tells us that if we think about unpleasant things, we feel bad, and if we think about pleasant things, we feel good. As we have already seen with the technique for making the most of your good memories, the way that we think about things has a big impact on the intensity of what we feel about them.

CASE study: Eliminating Anxiety

Part of John's job involved giving presentations, and he got very nervous about them. Before each one he would run movies in his head, with the aim of being "prepared for the worst." Because the movies were "shot" from his own point of view as presenter, he felt more anxious the more scenarios he imagined. When his colleague suggested he try viewing the mental movies as an objective observer, rather than a participant, he became much less anxious.

• John found that a detached point of view distanced him from unhelpful emotions.
• With practice, he could see his future self coping calmly with mishaps and tough questions. His presentations went better because he was less nervous.
• He found he could get even better results by imagining presentations that were well received, because mentally rehearsing success makes success more likely.

Alter Your Viewpoint

One of the most powerful ways to alter the impact of a mental image is to change the point of view from which you look at it. If you are viewing a memory from the point of view that you had when it happened, seeing it through your own eyes, you will find that you revisit the memory exactly as you remember it, and will probably also feel the emotion that goes with that memory. If, however, you take the point of view of an impartial observer, someone looking at the scene from the outside, so that rather than being yourself, you are seeing an image of yourself, you will find that you are automatically more detached from the accompanying emotion. You can reduce the emotion even more by sending the image farther away in your perceptual space, by draining the color out of it, and by making it dimmer, blurrier, or more faded. Practice this way of thinking regularly, so that when you really need to switch your viewpoint, you can do so easily.

TIP Altering your mental images is a skill that you can learn fairly quickly—emotionally neutral images are easier to practice on.

Defuse Problem Triggers

Like everyone else, you will undoubtedly have some triggers for automatic responses, but while many responses will be nearly universal—if you are out driving and you see a red light ahead, for example, it's likely that you, like every other driver, will find yourself automatically wanting to brake—others will be highly personalized and will be yours alone. You probably know what they are, but it is possible to learn some effective ways of defusing them and robbing them of their power over you. Some of the trigger-response pairings you have picked up along the way may be particularly unhelpful if they attach themselves to broader situations. For example, if, as a child, you originally started to feel anxious when you saw a frown on your parent's face, but now find that that anxiety is tapped by almost anyone frowning at you, from your boss to a parking attendant, you need to take some action to diminish the power of that particular trigger.

TECHNIQUES
to practice

Use this technique to get rid of an unwanted emotional response, or to defuse the trigger for a bad habit. It installs a fresh sequence of mental associations.

1 Take a mental picture of the "trigger" situation. What triggers the response?

2 Let go of that picture, and see yourself as you will be when you have overcome that problem. Make the picture bright and compelling, so you get a good feeling as you look at it.

3 Shrink the good picture to a powerful small image

4 Look at the "trigger" picture, this time with the positive image in a lower corner. Make the trigger picture disappear, and expand the positive image to full size, making a "Swisssh!" sound to emphasize the exchange.

5 Hold for a moment, then blank your mental screen.

6 Repeat five times in quick succession.

7 Look at the trigger picture again. You will find that your response to it is weaker.

Dealing with Your Inner Critic

Many people are held back from reaching their full potential by an inner voice, also known as the "chatterbox" or "gremlin," that constantly nags at them.

You can reduce the impact of this voice. Where is it coming from? Most people locate it in their heads. What does it say, and how do you feel about it? What kind of impact would it have if:

→ It was coming from your right big toe instead?
→ It had a very high-pitched voice?
→ It was louder? Or quieter?
→ It came from outside your body altogether?
→ It had the voice of a well-known cartoon character?
→ It had a humorous tone, with a chuckle in its voice?
→ It had a kindly, nurturing tone?

Which one worked best for you? How does it feel to realize that you can change the impact that the inner critic has on how you feel? And when will this be most useful to you?

Everyone has an Inner Critic Although everyone has a voice that diminishes their confidence at times, how much attention you pay to your negative inner critic is entirely up to you—it's within your control.

Summary: Dealing with Problems

Turning problems over and over in your head can quickly become counterproductive, making a situation feel more difficult than it actually is. The key to dealing with problems is to stay focused on the solution, remain relaxed and positive, and not let your personal gremlins take control.

Plan of Action

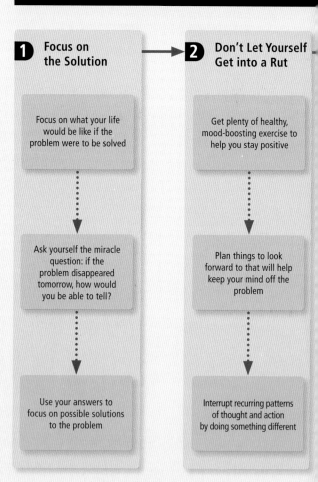

1 Focus on the Solution

Focus on what your life would be like if the problem were to be solved

Ask yourself the miracle question: if the problem disappeared tomorrow, how would you be able to tell?

Use your answers to focus on possible solutions to the problem

2 Don't Let Yourself Get into a Rut

Get plenty of healthy, mood-boosting exercise to help you stay positive

Plan things to look forward to that will help keep your mind off the problem

Interrupt recurring patterns of thought and action by doing something different

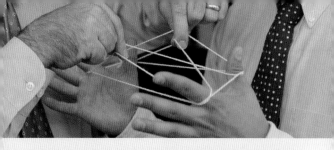

3 Alter Your Viewpoint

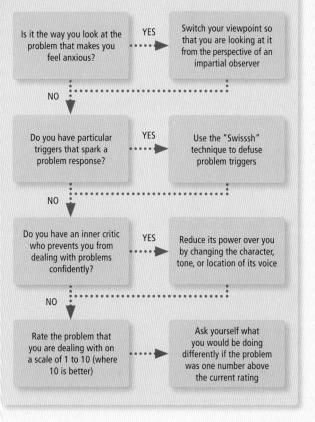

| Is it the way you look at the problem that makes you feel anxious? | YES ⋯▸ | Switch your viewpoint so that you are looking at it from the perspective of an impartial observer |

NO

| Do you have particular triggers that spark a problem response? | YES ⋯▸ | Use the "Swisssh" technique to defuse problem triggers |

NO

| Do you have an inner critic who prevents you from dealing with problems confidently? | YES ⋯▸ | Reduce its power over you by changing the character, tone, or location of its voice |

NO

| Rate the problem that you are dealing with on a scale of 1 to 10 (where 10 is better) | ⋯▸ | Ask yourself what you would be doing differently if the problem was one number above the current rating |

Deal with Other People

Sometimes it can seem as if life would be perfect if you didn't have to deal with the difficult people around you. But do those people think of themselves as difficult? Very few people deliberately set out to be awkward.

Keep an Objective View

Someone with whom you have a problem may be regarded as easygoing by someone else. Equally, you may sometimes appear to be the "difficult" one without realizing it. You show different aspects of yourself to your partner, your colleagues, your children, and your friends. What they perceive is their mental image of you, filtered by previous memories, associations, and their own beliefs about the type of person you are. This works both ways—so that when you have a problem with somebody, you are really having a problem with your image of them.

Every Dispute has Three Viewpoints

When you are locked in any kind of conflict with someone else, it is hard to keep the mental flexibility to find creative ways to resolve it. The stronger your emotion, the more rigid and set your thinking tends to become. The key to remaining flexible enough to give yourself more choice

think SMART

Look at a recent disagreement from each of the three viewpoints, starting with your own.

B careful to let go of any feelings from one viewpoint before stepping into the next. To get the best out of this exercise, mark out the three viewpoints as separate places in the room, and physically move from one to another. After viewing the dispute from the detached overview position, what advice would you give to the "you" in the first viewpoint?

How the Viewpoints Work

Teach yourself to switch between different viewpoints flexibly in order to gain the broadest possible view of any situation. Each viewpoint has its own advantages and disadvantages.

Advantages and Disadvantages

ADVANTAGES	DISADVANTAGES
Your own point of view: Good for knowing what you want, knowing how you feel about things, and for standing your ground firmly.	**Your own point of view:** Can lead to selfishness or arrogance; you may lack awareness of how you appear, and use others for your own ends.
The other person's point of view: Good for seeing clearly what the other person wants, and for empathy; may help you to see how you appear to them.	**The other person's point of view:** Can lead to passive behavior, or, in extreme cases, a martyred approach in which you see others' viewpoints so clearly that you always put them first.
A detached overview: Good for looking at things objectively, calming down, seeing the interaction as a whole system, and noting its wider consequence.	**A detached overview:** Lacking understanding of how the participants in the situation feel. This viewpoint can lead you to come across as cold.

about your response is to practice looking at the conflict from three different viewpoints: your own, the other person's, and a detached overview.

Bring Wisdom to Conflicts
Getting stuck in any one of these three positions, so that you only see the situation from one point of view, has disadvantages. Wisdom comes from being able to move freely between the viewpoints, and in being able to let go of the feelings arising from one viewpoint before moving to another, so you can see the situation with fresh eyes.

Deal with Criticism

How do you respond to critical comments? Do you take them to heart, or stop them at arm's length and examine them to see if they are true? How about compliments? Do you treat them in the same way, or differently?

Treat Criticism as Feedback

It is very common for people to take criticism immediately to heart, whether it is well founded or not, but to hold compliments at a distance until they have analyzed them. A more successful recipe for happiness is to do the opposite—to accept compliments freely while subjecting criticisms to careful scrutiny. To extract the useful learning from a critical remark, follow this simple two-step process:

- Mentally detach yourself from the emotional impact of the criticism. Imagine you are rising above the person making the criticism and looking down at them.
- Ask yourself: "What do I need to learn from this?"

You may find that you learn as much about the person offering the criticism as you do about yourself.

Stay Positive A mature attitude to criticism—that it is invaluable feedback—is a useful tool in life. Instead of becoming defensive when criticized, aim to remain open to comment, and to analyze it calmly.

Be Aware of Projection

"Projection" is a therapy term that describes the perception of your own feelings in another person, without the realization that your interpretation is really about you.

Assume for a moment that the reason you are able to recognize a quality you dislike in someone else is because you have some of that quality yourself. This idea works both ways—even if you don't realize it, it means that you also have at least traces of the qualities that you admire in other people.

Difficult people make the best teachers

Use Problematic People as Practice

Everyone, no matter how obnoxious they seem, is acting from a positive intention toward themselves. Viewing "difficult" people from this perspective makes it easier to understand them. Take this principle one step further and realize that they are giving you an opportunity to learn. Some of the most valuable lessons you have learned will have come from learning to handle difficult people—perhaps a grumpy colleague who unknowingly gave you practice in drawing a person out of themselves. Try running through this exercise a few times, using a different person as your example each time, to increase your understanding:

→ Think of a person who does something that irritates you, or behaves in a way that you don't like.

→ What is the positive intention behind their behavior? See yourself briefly though their eyes. What do you learn from this different viewpoint?

→ If that person's behavior had a positive intention toward you behind it, what would that positive intention be? What positive lessons do you need to learn from your interaction with that person?

→ Ask yourself: "How am I like that person? When do I behave like that?"

4

Create
the Vision
You Want

Now that you are clear about your values and have loosened any limiting beliefs, you can firm up your goals and bring them to life in a way that will enlist your unconscious mind to help make it happen. Installing a vibrant image of your goal into your future will turbocharge your motivation and keep you focused on doing whatever it takes to achieve them. This section guides you through:

- Why setting goals is important
- What works in goal-setting
- The five conditions of successful goals
- How to make your goal compelling
- How to install goals into your future

Set Your Goals

Without goals you would just be drifting aimlessly, at the mercy of whatever events come along in your life. You need to have a clear idea about where you want to be in order to take the action needed to get there.

Use Goals to Give You Direction

By contrast, when you know what your goals are, you know the path you have to follow to get there—and you have something to aim at, so you can make corrections if you get blown off course. A sense of purpose is a fundamental human need. Without purpose or meaning in your life, you become unhappy—as you will know if you have spent any length of time in an unfulfilling job. With goals, you become more flexible and resilient and better able to cope with changing conditions as you continually develop.

Free Mental Energy

If you find it hard to think of activities that would be enjoyable, you need to free some mental energy. Cut out activities that may be pleasurable, but don't offer you enjoyment. Cutting down on television watching would be a good start. Switch off a soap opera you watch regularly and you'll already have freed up five hours a week that you could spend enriching your relationships with real people.

Look to the Future

Assess where you are now

Fix on your long-term goals over a set time period

Halfway through the period you have set, assess your progress

Adjust your medium-term goals if necessary. Fix on your next set of long-term goals

Choose Enjoyment over Pleasure

After extensive research, the psychologist Mihaly Csikszentmihalyi concluded that we are happiest in "flow" states, in which we are completely absorbed in what we are doing. Characteristic of a flow state is the focus that comes from having a defined goal. The stretch we find in going for an ambitious goal gives us enjoyment, and enjoyment is different from pleasure, which is merely the feeling of contentment we get whenever we satisfy biological or socially conditioned expectations—with alcohol, drugs, or material possessions. Pleasure leaves us unchanged; enjoyment is a sign that we are growing and developing. Some examples would be:

→ Making a success of a crucial presentation
→ Training for and running a marathon
→ Reading an inspirational book that changes your point of view

Boost Your Self-Esteem

A psychology study at Washington University in St. Louis found that people's self-esteem varies according to whether on a typical day they think mostly about the past, the present, or the future. People with high self-esteem who feel good most of the time focus mainly on positive events in the future, while people with low self-esteem and a lot of negative feelings think more about unpleasant events in the past. If you feel you have learned from past events, you will find it easier to move on and not dwell on aspects that didn't work and which you now cannot change. Learning from life as you go is an effective way to avoid retrospective regrets about "what might have been."

TIP Try out new, exciting experiences to get ideas and broaden your horizons. Sometimes you don't know what you want until you've tried it.

Make Goal-Setting Work

Changing your habits is not easy—years of practice will have embedded them into your neural circuitry. In order to overcome the inertia that we are all familiar with, it's essential to have a clear vision of where you want to be.

Engage Your Unconscious Mind

When you have a vision that you can see, hear, and feel, it engages you on more than just an intellectual level. It gives you the emotional motivation you will need to get through setbacks and overcome inertia. Setting a goal in the right way offers a template or "attractor" for your unconscious mind, which sets up the attention mechanisms in your brain to notice the people and opportunities that can help you get closer to where you want to be. It also allows you to evaluate the changes in your surroundings so that you will be aware of whether you are getting closer to your desired outcome, or moving farther away from it.

Distinguish between Goals and Feelings

"I want to be happy" is not a goal. You can be happy right now, for at least a short while, by bringing to mind a happy time in your life, or a person you like. This happens instantly and is accomplished by your internal response to happy or positive thoughts. Goals, by contrast, involve changes in the external world around you—you actually have to make something happen to achieve most goals, and this will take time.

Feelings versus Goals

FEELING OR VALUE (such as "happiness")	GOAL (such as "promoted by the end of this year")
Vague	Specific
You can have it now	It will take time to achieve
No steps or planning required	Steps are needed to get there
Abstract	Measurable

Envisaging Your Goals

It may be that you have known for a long time what your goals are. Alternatively, you may have started with only a vague notion that you want things to be different from how they have been up to now.

If your goals are not yet as clear as you would like them to be, here are some ways of getting started:

→ Title three sheets of paper with "Things that I want more of," "Things that I want to keep as they are," and "Things that I want less of." Divide each sheet into two columns and write as many entries as you can in the left-hand column, with your reasons for each entry in the right-hand column.

→ Think about people you admire. What is it that you admire? How could you be more like them?

→ A feeling can be a starting point for drawing up your goals. If you want to be happier, what achievable changes would make it easy for you to be happy?

→ Images may be easier to work with than words. Use magazine pictures that appeal to you to create a collage representing your goal.

Sample List Writing down what you want more of, and why you want it, will help you to consolidate your goals.

Things I want more of:
- Spare time to spend with my kids
- Playing golf
- Challenging work projects

Why?:
- They are only young for a short time
- Exercise and fun
- To show what I have to offer

Free Up Your Energy by Decluttering

We are all affected by our surroundings to some extent, and the environment we create for ourselves mirrors our inner state of mind. A cluttered space will drain your energy.

Clearing superfluous clutter is one easy way to give your energy a boost and to start freeing yourself from past baggage so you can look to the future.

Decluttering is easy once you get started

→ Start with the small stuff. To get past the feeling of being overwhelmed, start with your junk drawer. It will inspire you to move on to the bigger stuff.

→ Clear out anything not used or loved. Under normal circumstances, if you have not used an item in the past year, then you will not use it again.

→ Set yourself a time limit. If you have something that is unfinished or needing repair, set yourself a period of time to get it fixed. If by then it's still unfinished, it has to go!

→ Recycle items that are "too good to throw out." It is not easy for most people to just throw something away—so recycle it to friends, schools, or charities who will actually use it.

→ "One in, one out." Once you have cleared, maintain that clutter-free state with a rule that you clear space for whatever you bring into your home by clearing out something else.

→ Get started! The moment you start, you will feel lighter and empowered to continue. Other people around you will be motivated to clear their clutter. Your home or workspace will feel the benefits and appear full of positive energy.

TIP **Set your goals at the right level. If you never achieve any of them, your sights are set too high; if you always achieve all of them, they are set too low.**

Distinguish between "Need" and "Want"

Philosophies such as Buddhism talk about the need for non-attachment to the results you get, so that you don't get upset if things do not work out the way you wanted. In fact, being attached to a goal—needing it to happen—arises when you have a mental image of the goal, but also another mental image, of not reaching the goal, which is at least as strong. You may not be consciously aware of the negative image—but it is always there. The "away from" motivation that this creates will get in the way of achieving the goal. By contrast, when you want your goal to happen but you will be composed if it does not, you only have a positive mental image. Your motivation will be "toward," which is more directed and less stressful.

Use S.M.A.R.T. Goals with Care

If you are in business you will probably have come across the S.M.A.R.T. approach, which states that goals should be Specific, Measurable, Achievable, Realistic and Timed. These are all necessary criteria for success, but they leave out an important factor: do you care whether you achieve the goal? In the environment where the S.M.A.R.T. approach originated there was no shortage of "away from" motivation. If you did not carry out your tasks, you would be fired. When you are setting goals for yourself, you need an approach that engages your unconscious mind and harnesses the power of "toward" motivation.

5 minute FIX

In a situation in which you need to assess motivation fast before you act, make a quick check.

You can establish that you are using the right—"toward"—motivation by asking yourself:

- What will this goal gain for me?
- Will I lose anything if I reach my goal?

Your gains should be greater than your losses, and should be placed firmly in the future.

Find a Route to Successful Goals

By now you will have some goals in mind. You may have had defined outcomes all along; if not, they will have become clearer as you worked on your values or worked through the envisaging process on the previous pages.

Create a Checklist

There are many different formulas for goal-setting checklists. One of the most effective, both for precision and for engaging your emotional commitment, is the formula known as the P.O.W.E.R. process. Go through the letters of the word "Power" step by step, as described on the following pages. You are finding out if your goal will meet the criteria that tell you that it is achievable.

POWER—the Keywords

P	Positive thinking
O	Own your goal
W	specify What and When
E	consider all the Effects
R	ensure that the Route is known and feasible

P—Positive Thinking

This is about the need to be careful with the words you use when you write your goal down, and even when you think to yourself about it. Setting a goal gives your unconscious a target to work toward. This acts as a set of instructions for deciding what aspects of your environment are worth giving attention to—which events, things, and people you will decide to notice because they could help you to reach your goal, and which will not make it onto your radar because they are irrelevant. Remember that the unconscious does not recognize a negative. So if you state your goal as "I don't want to be in this unfulfilling job a year from now," the mental image you have from this wording is still of the current, unfulfilling job.

Get the Job Done

Making sure you keep the word "not" out of your goal statement is not

Release Your Power A clear vision of your goals is the key to accessing the full energy of your internal drive.

enough by itself. Your could restate your goal as "I want to be out of this job in a year." This takes "not" out of the equation, but it is still a statement of what you want to get away from. It is incomplete, because it says nothing about what you want to move toward. Your unconscious is a precise instrument: usually it will do its best to fulfill exactly what you ask of it—but no more. If in a year you are unemployed, whatever you are consciously thinking, your unconscious will regard the result as a job completed, because it has given you exactly what you asked. You need to modify your goal statement to ensure that your unconscious understands your end aim:

"In a year, I want to be in a job that pays better, is more enjoyable, and has better prospects."

While this is not yet specific enough to be a well-formed goal statement, at least it is now pointing you in the right direction for action.

O—Own Your Goal

Whose goal is it? You will only be truly engaged with it if it is yours. If you are trying to live up to someone else's idea of who you should be, you are bound to have some unconscious resistance—unless your vision for yourself exactly coincides with theirs. Ownership is also about being able to bring the goal about by your own actions. It would be pointless to set "winning the lottery" as a goal, because once you have bought a ticket, the outcome is entirely out of your hands. What answers do you get to these questions:

- What can I do to bring this goal about by my own actions?
- What can I do to influence the outcome?
- What do I need to do to achieve this goal?

W—Specify What and When

Now you need to make sure your goal is expressed precisely, because whatever you ask for is exactly what your unconscious mind will work to provide for you. Define the goal so that both your intellect and your unconscious mind know exactly what you want and begin to work cooperatively to get it for you.

- Make sure the goal is quantifiable
- What will be different when you have your goal?

Taking money as an example, "I want to be richer" is not a well-formed goal. How much richer? What form will that wealth be in? If your goal is to have a certain income, is that after taxes or before? If your goal is to buy a new house, where will that house be? How many rooms? What criteria will the location have to satisfy? Write all these points down. Then make a sensory image of your goal. In your imagination, put yourself in the situation of having the goal. See it through your own eyes, as vividly as you can.

> **Be careful what you wish for.**
>
> Traditional Chinese saying

Make sure that you have detailed and satisfactory answers to all of the following questions, and that you have a clear picture of your goal in your mind's eye. Fill in colors, sounds, and scents as you go:

- Where are you?
- Who else is there?
- What are you doing?
- What do you see, hear, feel, taste, and smell now that you have your goal?

> **The more distinct a goal is, the simpler it will be to achieve**

This detailed visualization performs three functions. It brings the mental image of your goal to life in a way that words on their own never could, so you begin to get the emotional response that is essential for motivation. It gives your unconscious mind a sensory-rich template, so that it has a very definite target to aim at. And it gives you information about what life will be like when you have achieved your goal, so that you can make any adjustments you need to make sure that this is what you really want.

TECHNIQUES
to practice

As you work toward your goal, use this exercise regularly to check your progress.

Every goal needs an "achieve by" date. If you do not set a date, your goal will always remain in the future.

1 Set a target date for your goal.
2 Choose several dates between now and the date you have set, and write them in your planner.
3 On each of these staged dates, ask yourself what you have done to get closer to your goal, and write down what you have already achieved.
4 If you find that you are hitting the set dates without making progress, make a detailed check of your motivation: you may be sabotaging your own progress.

E—Consider All the Effects

Although your goal may be about a particular area of your life, it will affect other areas. Consider the consequences of achieving your goal for every other area of your life; when you have, you can be sure you really want it.

What will it cost you to achieve the goal? Sometimes there are costs to achieving a goal, in terms of time, effort, or what you will have to give up. Ask these questions to make sure your goal is worth the sacrifices:

- What will happen when I have it?
- What won't happen when I have it?
- Are there any downsides to achieving it?

What are the wider effects of achieving your goal? Any significant goal will have an impact on the balance of your life—think this through now to avoid unforeseen consequences later.

- How will this goal affect the people I care about?
- How will this goal affect the wider communities of which I am a part?

CASE study: Finding a Life Balance

Karl was totally focused on building his cell phone retail business, setting a goal to become a millionaire before he was 30. He succeeded—but he worked such long hours to achieve it that his relationship was in trouble, and he was in danger of burning out. When a checkup revealed a heart murmur, he reluctantly began to delegate some of his workload and set aside some time for exercise. To his surprise, even with his new work habits, his business continued to grow, although at a more moderate and sustainable pace.

- *In balancing his life better, Karl learned to enjoy life and, suffering less from stress, was easier to be around. Although his relationship did not survive, his quality of life did improve.*
- *He found his increased mental alertness helped him to come up with more original business ideas.*

Looking ahead to Your Goal

HIGH IMPACT

- Anticipating how the goal will feel when you achieve it
- Looking realistically at any disadvantages it may have
- Checking your unconscious for any negative signals

NEGATIVE IMPACT

- Assuming that once you have the goal, life will be perfect
- Concentrating purely on the advantages of the goal
- Ignoring any doubts coming from your unconscious

How much do you want this goal? If you are not committed to your goal, you will not achieve it. If you feel doubt, your unconscious may be telling you that something needs more attention.

- How do I feel about this goal?
- Do I want it 100 percent?
- Does my energy increase when I think about it?

If you answered "no" to any question, adjust the goal until you feel enthusiastic about it.

R—Ensure that the Route Is Known

At this stage, it is enough to have a feeling that the goal is possible. How you get there will be easier to work out later, after you have placed the goal in your future.

- Has anyone else achieved this goal? Then why not you?
- Who can assist you in getting there?

If no one has achieved a similar goal before:

- What resources do you have that will help?
- What additional resources do you need?
- What can you learn from any previous attempts? Once your goal meets the P.O.W.E.R. criteria, you are ready to install it into your future.

TIP Think about what you will learn and how you will grow in the journey toward your goal, as well as the benefits when you have achieved it.

Summary: Set POWERful Goals

Goals give you direction and purpose. They help you identify and focus on your priorities, a vital process if you are to know where you want to go in your life and what steps you need to take to get there. But it is important to choose and define your goals with care; weak, hazy, or negative goals merely give the impression of forward movement—and can obstruct your progress. The P.O.W.E.R. checklist— which stands for Positivity, Ownership, What/When, Effects, and Route—will help you turn vague wants and desires into definite, focused, and achievable goals.

Plan of Action

P **Think Positively**

Envision a set of goals that show you where you want to be in the future

O **Own Your Goals**

Check that you wish to achieve each goal for your own sake, not for anyone else

W **Specify What and When**

Visualize yourself having achieved each goal—this will help you define it more clearly

E **Consider All the Effects**

Ask yourself what it will cost to achieve each goal

R **Think about the Route**

Ask yourself what resources you need to achieve the goal

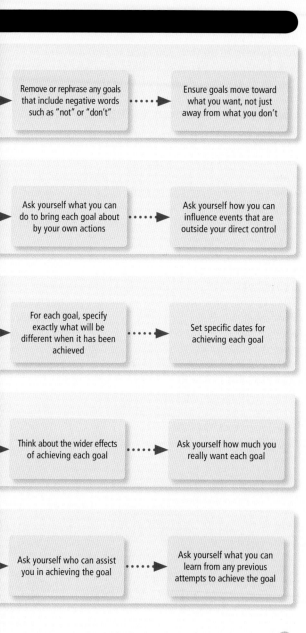

Remove or rephrase any goals that include negative words such as "not" or "don't" ‥‥‥▶ Ensure goals move toward what you want, not just away from what you don't

Ask yourself what you can do to bring each goal about by your own actions ‥‥‥▶ Ask yourself how you can influence events that are outside your direct control

For each goal, specify exactly what will be different when it has been achieved ‥‥‥▶ Set specific dates for achieving each goal

Think about the wider effects of achieving each goal ‥‥‥▶ Ask yourself how much you really want each goal

Ask yourself who can assist you in achieving the goal ‥‥‥▶ Ask yourself what you can learn from any previous attempts to achieve the goal

Place the Goal in Your Future

Now that your goal is defined, you need to install it into your future. To do this, you need to find out which direction in your perceptual space signifies "future" to you, to engage your whole brain in the goal installation.

Help Your Unconscious to Organize Time

Because we can't see time, we tend to use spatial metaphors to think and talk about it. We use expressions like "the distant past," "the short term," and "the far future." The idea of time as being a linear sequence of events, in which one moment follows another, will feel quite familiar to you. This is how your unconscious mind organizes your past memories—events that happened a long time ago feel farther away than something that happened yesterday, and two hundred years in the future is "a long way off" compared to your plans for tomorrow. You also talk about time as having a particular direction relative to your viewpoint—for example, "I've put it behind me," or "I'm looking forward to the summer." You are used to seeing graphs where time goes from left to right along the lower axis—if you saw one with the future moving toward you, or with time moving from right to left, it would appear strange to you because time would appear to be "shifting" in the wrong direction.

Looking at Your Timeline

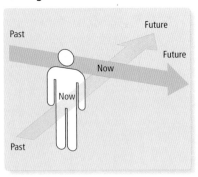

Think about how you visualize time, and your own positioning on your timeline. Two common directions for timelines are shown on the left. If you are moving toward a partially achieved goal, you are more likely to see yourself already on the timeline's path.

Discover Your Timeline

We are not usually consciously aware of our sense of the future's direction, but it is very easy to discover it, and being able to visualize it clearly will help your future seem more real to you.

→ Think about time as being like a line, where one moment follows another. The past is at one end of the line, the future at the other, and "now" is somewhere in between.
→ As you look at that line, which direction is the past?
→ Which direction is the future?
→ Notice where "now" is: where you are, or ahead of you?
→ Join the past, present, and future with a line, and notice where that line is in relation to you.

What color is your timeline? The color has no particular significance, but it will help you to see the timeline more clearly.

Choose Your Direction

Timelines most commonly take one of two forms:

- The future is in front of you, the past is behind you, and you are standing at "now"—this form makes it easy to be "in the moment."
- The future is to your right, the past is to your left, now is a little in front of you—this form can be helpful for time management and punctuality issues, as you can see where events are in relation to each other.

These are not the only possibilities—timelines have no right or wrong directions. Take the form that comes naturally in a situation, and use it in your visualizations.

TIP If you do not see your timeline clearly, it does not matter, provided you have a sense of which direction the future is in, and where "now" is.

Make Your Goal Compelling

The final step before installing your goal is to make your mental image of the goal as vivid as possible. You want a picture that is so compelling that it pulls you toward it without your having to try to motivate yourself. To do this, tune up the image to appeal to all of your senses.

- Turn up the visual qualities of the image. Make it vivid and compelling but not garish, as it has to remain realistic to maximize its emotional impact. Then step into it (if you are not there already) so that you are seeing it as if you were really there.

- Turn up the sound and the sensations. What do you hear? What does it feel like to have achieved your goal—and to know you deserved it? Make any final adjustments that you need to, and turn up those good feelings even more.

- Now step back out of the picture. If you stayed in it, you could daydream about the goal forever without doing anything about it. Stepping out reminds you that you are not there yet—and you have to make things happen in the real world in order to get there.

TECHNIQUES
to practice

Use your timeline as a tool in this effective technique for fast relaxation

You should find that it will help you to take yourself out of uncomfortable emotions, and will give you some perspective if you need to make a tough decision.

1 Close your eyes and become aware of your timeline.

2 Allow yourself to float above "now," or let the timeline sink away beneath you.

3 Float up until you reach a height at which you are comfortable.

4 Notice how you feel floating above the timeline, compared to being at timeline level.

5 When you feel relaxed, float down and open your eyes.

Creating Your Vision

Experiencing your goal as if it has already happened makes it real to you and strengthens your feeling that it is not only possible, but is definitely going to happen.

See Yourself in the Picture As you look at your image of the goal, you should feel a powerful motivating pull to get there.

Specify Who Is There with You Seeing who will be with you in your future will increase your emotional connection with the goal.

Make Sure the Picture Is Bright A big, bright, compelling image will engage your heart as well as your intellect.

TIP If your goal is not motivating enough, make sure that it meets all the P.O.W.E.R. criteria and experiment with making it more vivid.

Install Your Goal

"Planting" a goal into your future timeline makes it part of the landscape of your unconscious mind, and will give you a feeling of certainty that your goal is going to happen—your unconscious will treat it as though it already has. The installation can be a very powerful process emotionally, which has the benefit of embedding your goal strongly in your memory and your thoughts. Make sure that your goal meets the P.O.W.E.R. criteria and is as vivid as possible before you install it.

Combine Your Conscious and Unconscious

The process is designed to work on both a conscious and an unconscious level. You may find that ideas and images about how to achieve the goal start coming to you either during the installation process or shortly afterward. Any ritual consistent with your belief system that you wish to perform before the installation, such as saying a prayer or breathing life into the picture of your goal, can only help to make the process more significant for you.

think SMART

You may find that floating your goal into your timeline—an equally valid alternative method—works better for you.

Some people find this variation on the process described opposite is an easier way to install their goal into their future.

1 Float forward above the timeline into the future, carrying your goal with you.

2 Release the goal above the target date. Let it float down into the timeline and embed itself as part of your future.

3 Float back to now, watching events between now and the target date realigning themselves to help you reach your goal.

Placing Your Goal in Your Timeline

You can follow this process on your own or, even better, get a friend to guide you through each step, leaving you free to experience your thoughts and feelings as you go.

Before you start, lay your timeline out on the floor, making sure you have enough space to take a step beyond the point that represents the date by which you are going to achieve your goal.

→ Put your image of your goal into an imaginary frame, and as you hold it, step onto the timeline, facing the future.

→ Walk along the timeline into the future, carrying your goal. Stop when the goal is directly above the target date. Let go of the goal and allow it to settle into your timeline.

→ Step forward into the goal and experience it fully—allow yourself to feel the sense of achievement.

→ Take a step beyond your goal and turn around so that you are looking back at the successful achievement of your goal. You may notice that the events leading up to the achievement realign themselves to support the achievement. What advice do you have for the "you" back at "now"?

Return to "now" along the timeline, and look into the future. You will have a sense of knowing that the goal is going to happen.

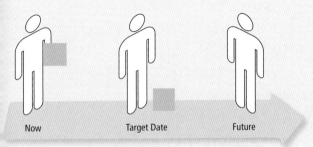

Now   Target Date   Future

Getting There
5

Now that you have set your goals, you have to get out there and make them happen! This can seem daunting—unless you clearly identify potential routes to your goal, and take steps to safeguard your energy and commitment along the way. This section shows you:

- Why it is important to write your goals down and make a public commitment
- Strategies for freeing up your energy and getting started
- How to create a detailed route to your goal
- How to stay motivated and learn from mistakes
- The benefits of looking beyond material and performance goals

Make Your Goals Happen

Even after your goals have been set, it's important to plan your route to them in manageable steps to ensure that you don't become discouraged by the task. This section shows you how to turn your ideas into reality.

Switch Off Your Autopilot

The results we get come from the way in which our actions work with our environment (the people around us, the resources available to us, and rules and expectations of society). We cannot control our environment, but we are able to choose our actions. So when you change your actions, your results change (not always predictably, which is why you need to monitor the results closely and make further changes if you need to). Most of your behavior happens on autopilot, without conscious analysis. This works well on a day-to-day level, since you would never have time to think through every single decision consciously. However, it presents a challenge when you want to change your behavior.

> **It takes at least 21 days to establish a new habit**

Stay Focused

Making behavioral change happen is often compared to the process of turning an oil tanker around. Old habits have their own momentum. They will reassert themselves as soon as your attention wanders, until your new habits have had time to become established. Remember that you need to keep your goals at the forefront of your mind.

> **One of the illusions of life is that the present hour is not the critical, decisive hour. Write it on your heart that every day is the best day of the year.**
>
> Ralph Waldo Emerson

Changing Your Behavior

Change can happen sooner than you expect. It does take time and effort, but you can make it a lot easier by doing it the smart way rather than the hard way.

→ **Write your goals down.** When you write your goals down, they become more real than when you only think about them, or even talk about them. Writing the goals fixes them in your memory and stops them from changing or fading away. As you write your goals, you activate the prefrontal cortex—a part of your brain that deals with expectations, decision-making, and choice—making you more able to notice and change habitual behaviors.

→ **Put your goals where you will see them every day**. Hang them on your bedroom wall, so that they are the first thing you see when you wake up; pin them in front of your desk at work; or have them as a start-up message or screensaver on your computer. Have them accessible at all times.

→ **Make a public commitment to your goals.** This takes your goals another step along the road from idea to reality. People are social animals, and you probably do care what other people think about them. Use that characteristic to help your motivation by telling people you trust and whose opinion you value about your goals.

Implementing Change

HIGH IMPACT

- Teaming up with a goal-setting partner to provide support
- Keeping your goals visible, and checking them every few days
- Discussing your goals with friends and colleagues

NEGATIVE IMPACT

- Trying—and failing—to make the journey on your own
- Writing your goals down, then putting them away in a drawer
- Keeping your goals to yourself and guarding them as your secret

Remember that You Have a Choice

In western societies, many people have had everything done for them as children, and had little early training in taking responsibility. During the teenage years, simple chores like doing the dishes become battlegrounds in the struggle for an independent identity. As an adult, this background can leave you with a feeling of resentment of any task you "have" to do. Even if the task is a vital step on the way to something you really want, you may find yourself doing it half-heartedly while inwardly complaining.

To get around this attitude, remind yourself that you are choosing your course of action. No one else is going to step in and do it for you. Do it gladly because it will take you closer to your goals.

Stay on Track

Displacement activities are what you do to avoid tackling some other more important task to which you have an unconscious resistance. An example might be checking your emails when you have a crucial report to write. The displacement activity is an attempt to reduce stress. It does not work, because at the back of your mind is the nagging feeling that there is something else you should be doing. You will find that the best way to reduce your stress levels is to get started on your most important task right away.

5 minute FIX

If you reach impasse on a task on the way to your goal, use this prompt.

The answers remind you why you need to act and should get you back on track fast.

- What part does this task play in my plan?
- In what way does it bring me closer to my goal?
- Visualize your goal coming closer as you complete the task, then get straight back to work.

TIP Walk like someone who is confident. It will change how you feel.

Give Yourself an Energy Boost

Our thoughts and emotions influence the physical systems of the body—and vice versa. If you stand slumped over, gazing at your shoes, you will find it hard to think positively—but the reverse is also true. What is your normal posture like, and how has it been influencing how you feel? What changes will you make from now on?

Straighten Up
Standing up with arms outspread, you'll find it easier to access positive thoughts and excitement.

Look Up It is hard to feel unhappy, low energy states when you are looking forward and out at the world.

Think Positive Keep the same position and let exciting thoughts flow through you. Experience them fully for a minute.

Focus on Your Desired Outcome

Most things become easier when you focus on the end result, rather than on the slog of getting there—it moves your way of thinking from passive to active, and closer to being at the Cause end of the spectrum.

Stay Clear about Your Goal

If you are working toward a long-term goal or goals, you may find that, over time, your focus gets blunted a little. If you discuss your goals with others, they may not always be supportive; other outside factors may raise doubts in your mind, and eventually your determination may begin to fail. You can stop this from happening along the way to your goal by maintaining a constant process of assessment. Even if your goal remains constant, other things— your personal circumstances or relationships, or the circumstances of people close to you—may change. Just because you may need to reconsider the route to your goal, though, don't falter, or lose focus. Go calmly back

CASE study: Speaking Up in Meetings

Kim, a marketing manager, found it hard to speak up in important meetings because she felt self-conscious. Yet in other areas of her work she was confident and focused. She realized that she was going into each meeting without a clear idea of what she wanted from it, even though the decisions to be made would have a major impact on her projects. After discussing the issue with her coach, she decided to get clear before each meeting on the way she wanted it to go. In the next meeting, Kim found herself speaking up to influence the outcome without even thinking about it.

• *Because she now had a desired outcome in mind, Kim's attention was directed outside herself in order to "read" the mood of the other participants, rather than inward to dwell on her sense of self-consciousness.*
• *She began to find that even outside work, people looked to her as a leader in most groups in which she found herself.*

over the steps to your goal and see if any of them need to change to take account of other changes.

Work Backward

Even when people have set a compelling goal for themselves, they may struggle with knowing where to start. Of all the possible actions that lie before you, which step should you take first? When you installed your goal on the timeline, some of the milestones along the way to your goal may have popped into your mind as you walked back to "now." To be sure you are clear about the best path to your goal, use the more left-brained approach shown in the flowchart on the right. It is based on the principle that you will find it easier to establish the route to your goal when you start from where you want to be, and work backward. Best of all, it offers you a clear path of action so that you know not only what comes first, but what comes next, too.

Milestones to Your Goal

Take a large sheet of paper and write your goal at the right-hand edge. Imagine that you have already achieved your goal.

Ask yourself what conditions needed to be in place before this goal happened in order for it to be achieved. Write each condition to the left of the goal.

Draw arrows joining the conditions to the goal. Treat each of these conditions as the result of some other previous conditions.

Ask "What conditions needed to be in place in order for this to happen?" Write them in their appropriate places to the left of the results.

Keep working backward until you arrive at your first step. You now have the essential "milestones" along the way to your goal.

Play to Your Strengths

Nobody can be a star at everything. Trying to follow someone else's formula for success can mean we try to become something we are not, and then blame ourselves when the formula turns out not to suit us.

Stay Aware

Remedying any gaps in your skills that hold you back, and facing the challenges of learning new ways of behaving can be extremely useful—but if that is all that you do, life will be a constant round of hard work, and you may find your motivation ebbing. Adaptation inevitably takes energy; to make your path to success sustainable, you also need to play to your strengths by using what you are naturally good at. The better you know yourself and the ways in which you are likely to respond in any situation, the easier it will be to choose the path that works for you.

- Notice which aspects of getting to your goal enthuse you, and which are more of a chore. If you can, find ways to make the chores easier by delegating them to someone else who is good at them. Remember, you are not required to do everything yourself.
- Make sure that all the actions necessary to achieve your goal are covered, by someone else if not by you—the temptation could be to neglect the ones that don't come naturally to you.

Using Help Effectively

HIGH IMPACT

- Facing up to all the tasks that must be done for you to achieve your goal
- Delegating where necessary
- Taking on those tasks for which you have a natural ability and enjoying working on them

NEGATIVE IMPACT

- Looking only at those tasks that you are confident you can do yourself
- Refusing to delegate any jobs
- Working on a host of tasks simultaneously and failing to enjoy any of them

Raise Your Self-Awareness

When your self-knowledge is strong, you become less likely to sabotage your efforts unconsciously, because you are familiar with how you think and operate. Use these questions to learn more about yourself.

→ **Do you recharge your energies by going out with lots of people, or by relaxing on your own or with a close friend or partner?** If the answer is "lots of people," your path to your goals needs to include plenty of opportunities for socializing or working in a group to keep your energy levels high. If the other option appeals more, make sure you build in some "me" time in which you can restore your energy.

> There may be several different paths to the same goal

→ **How do you know you are doing a good job?** Do you "just know" or do you need to hear it from other people? If you need lots of feedback, consider where you will be getting this from on the way to your goal—if you don't get enough, you may start to doubt your own abilities, and this doubt will in turn dilute the effort that you are putting in and make it harder for you to reach your goal. If you "just know," you may want to sound out a second opinion occasionally to get a balanced view of your progress, and to ensure that you stay on track and that your vision of the end goal remains clear.

→ **Are you more at ease with details, or with the big picture?** If you are a detail person, you may need deliberately to remind yourself of your ultimate goal from time to time so you don't get lost in the trivia of day-to-day living, and mired down in the minutiae of everyday life. If you are more interested in the big picture, it may be wise to enlist the help of someone else to check the details for you in case you have missed something.

Deal with Overload

Sometimes there just seems to be too much to do, and big projects can seem overwhelming. If you have followed the previous guidelines, this shouldn't happen often, but here's how to deal with it when it does.

Don't Do too Much

If you have too many projects going at once, you will have to make some choices about which ones you are going to complete, and which you want to put on the back burner. Refer back to your "six year, three year, one year" goal sheet to remind you of your priorities. Get into the habit of saying no to any new projects until you have your current commitments under control. If a task seems too big and overwhelming to get started, break it down into smaller tasks until you reach a size that you are comfortable with. Keep your end goal in mind and remember that each smaller task is another step toward it.

Manage Your Project Break big tasks down as if you were building a house—divide them into manageable stages and deal with them one by one.

TECHNIQUES
to practice

Use a system that works for getting things done: learn not to procrastinate.

When you fail to take action, it's usually because you don't want to take on a chore. You notice that a chore needs doing, think about how boring doing it will be, decide not to do it yet, then go around the same loop until you can't put off doing it any longer. This takes more energy than doing it right away. Use this technique whenever you feel yourself begin to procrastinate.

1 Take your least favorite chore.

2 Imagine how good things will be when you have completed the task, and how good you will feel as a result.

3 Keeping this image in mind, give five minutes of your full attention to the task and see how far you get.

Get Things in Perspective

Use your timeline to help you put your work into perspective and gain an overall focus on what you have to do. Mentally, lay your timeline out on the floor, with the project start and end dates marked out on it. Step away from your timeline and give yourself enough distance to see the task in the context of the time before it started and the time after it is complete. This will give you a more accurate perspective on it and reduce your feelings of "overwhelm" until you have your current commitments under control, and have time to think about whether you have the space to take on more.

Keep your commitment levels in mind at all times

TIP Leave some uncommitted "contingency time" for things you have overlooked or that need fixing unexpectedly—don't fill your schedule completely.

Summary: Making Goals Happen

Achieving your goals takes commitment and focus—but with a properly planned route and realistic, manageable stages, the process should not feel too overwhelming. Play to your strengths, but don't neglect the less enjoyable steps or stages along the way; with outside help, advice, or training, you can almost always overcome any personal limitations. If you make a start, everything else will soon fall into place.

Plan of Action

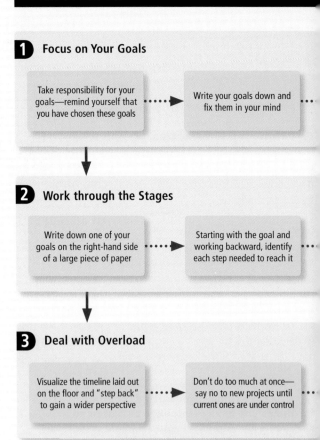

1 Focus on Your Goals

Take responsibility for your goals—remind yourself that you have chosen these goals ••••▶ Write your goals down and fix them in your mind ••••

2 Work through the Stages

Write down one of your goals on the right-hand side of a large piece of paper ••••▶ Starting with the goal and working backward, identify each step needed to reach it ••••

3 Deal with Overload

Visualize the timeline laid out on the floor and "step back" to gain a wider perspective ••••▶ Don't do too much at once—say no to new projects until current ones are under control ••••

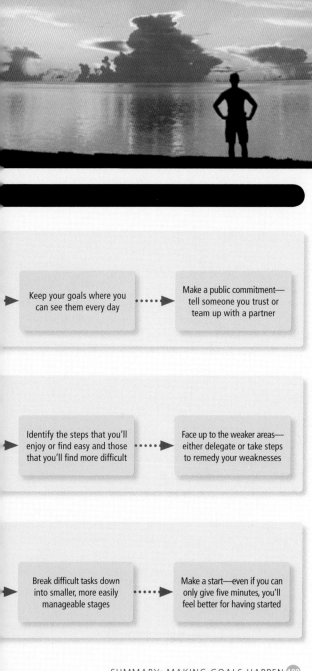

Keep your goals where you can see them every day ┈┈▶ Make a public commitment—tell someone you trust or team up with a partner

Identify the steps that you'll enjoy or find easy and those that you'll find more difficult ┈┈▶ Face up to the weaker areas—either delegate or take steps to remedy your weaknesses

Break difficult tasks down into smaller, more easily manageable stages ┈┈▶ Make a start—even if you can only give five minutes, you'll feel better for having started

Live Up to Your Self-Image

Psychologists have found that people tend to act in line with their self-image. If you see yourself as an achievement-oriented person, you are more likely to take the actions that will lead to achievement.

Make a Start

You will find that as soon as you take a small step in the direction you want to go, you will being to see yourself as that kind of person. For example, if you haven't been able to face clearing out the clutter in your home, you can get yourself started by committing to clearing out just one drawer—and then actually doing it. This makes it likely that you will go on and clear out more clutter—if not right away, then the following day. It also gives you a reference experience of keeping a commitment to yourself, so that you start to see yourself as a person who delivers on your promises. Like any other belief, self-image becomes a self-fulfilling prophecy that makes it easier to take action toward your goals in the future. The more reference experiences you create, the more you believe in yourself as an achiever.

Once a start has been made, the job will soon be completed

Watch Yourself Change

One of the ways in which many people make themselves feel bad is by perpetually comparing their performance with that of someone else, and finding themselves lacking. A more effective way of monitoring your performance is to compare where you are now with where you used to be, and notice how far you have come and the progress that you have made.

TIP Rather than compare yourself with people you admire, let them inspire you.

Reinforce Your Motivation

Psychologists and animal trainers have found that the most effective way to help both humans and animals form new habits is to reward and reinforce getting things right, rather than punishing mistakes.

You can use this principle to sustain your motivation.

→ When you are learning a new skill or practicing new behaviors, focus on the improvements over your previous performance, rather than giving yourself a hard time about any mistakes or omissions.

→ Reward yourself for reaching each milestone to keep your motivation high—you do not have to wait until you've achieved the final goal to start to feel good about it!

→ Take a moment at the end of each day to notice what has happened to bring you closer to your goal. This provides behavioral reinforcement to your unconscious mind, letting it know that it is on the right track and encouraging it to do more of the same.

Envisage Yourself as a Winner
Picture yourself as a success, and it is more likely that you will become one.

Take Care of Yourself

The journey to reach your goals may be long, and some times will be easier than others. In order to get there you need to make wise use of everything you have, especially of your most precious resource, your energy.

Be Kind to Your Body

You can make a difference to your mood and emotional stability. One of the most effective ways is to give up coffee. Caffeine (also present in smaller doses in tea, cola, and chocolate) mimics the effect of adrenaline to give you an energy surge followed by a dip. This can have a roller coaster effect on your emotions. Sugary foods have a similar effect. If you do decide to reduce your caffeine levels, do it gradually, reducing your intake in increments of one cup per day, to avoid the headaches that sometimes accompany an abrupt withdrawal.

TECHNIQUES *to* practice

Learn to use your unconscious to help you drop bad habits and address their underlying causes.

Establish what purpose your unconscious thinks these behaviors are serving. When you find this, it will be easier to give the habits up.

1 Close your eyes, still your mind, and call up an image representing the habit. It may be the little voice that nags you into wanting another cigarette, for example.

2 Thank the image for communicating with you. If you have a dislike of your own habit, this may be tough— remember, your unconscious wishes the best for you.

3 Ask the image what it is trying to do for you. Wait for its answer, which may arrive as a thought or an image.

4 Think of other ways of achieving the same end, without the drawbacks. Check that they are as effective at fulfilling the good intention behind the bad habit.

Maintain Your Energy

HIGH IMPACT

- Thinking long-term—eating well and exercising regularly to keep your energy stable
- Recognizing energy dips and balancing your activities to minimize them
- Ensuring that you consistently get enough sleep to awake refreshed each morning and remain alert through the day

NEGATIVE IMPACT

- Using quick fixes—sugar, caffeine or nicotine—to maintain your energy levels
- Ignoring energy dips and working straight through them, to the point of exhaustion
- Maintaining erratic sleeping habits, and treating either tiredness or sleeplessness with medication

Learn to Interpret Your Symptoms

Unhealthy lifestyles are a contributing factor to many illnesses. Sometimes physical symptoms can be early warning signs that your lifestyle needs to change. Stress headaches may be a sign that you are working too hard, persistent indigestion may be indicating that a change of diet is needed, and so on. If you ignore these symptoms or simply suppress them with over-the-counter medication, the warning message may be re-sent in a way that is harder to ignore. As well as consulting your physician when symptoms appear, you have nothing to lose by asking yourself (or the part of the body where the symptom appears): "If this is a message for me, what is it trying to tell me?" When you get an answer that makes sense to you, act on it. It is much better to make a small adjustment to your lifestyle now, than to risk a major change forced by illness farther down the line.

The name of the game is taking care of yourself, because you're going to live long enough to wish you had.

Grace Mirabella

Learn from Your Mistakes

Unless you are very lucky, not every single step along the path to your goal will go smoothly. Deal with mistakes and unforeseen problems by looking on them as opportunities from which you can learn.

Take Problems in Stride

When something does not turn out as you expected, ask yourself: "What do I need to learn from this?" and create some mental space for the answer to come to you. Asking this question means that you will learn from mistakes. If you choose not to learn from a particular mistake, life will keep sending you more opportunities to learn that lesson until you understand what it is trying to tell you.

Remain Realistic

One sure-fire way not to learn from the lessons that life gives us is to pretend that there are no problems at all. Sometimes, when things are going well, it can seem as though that is the case. But if you believe that everything must be perfect, the temptation is to ignore any signs that

think
SMART
!

Stay on track and avoid unpleasant surprises by making a "minesweep" from time to time, to check for anything that could knock you off course.

The function of a minesweep is to alert you to any changed circumstances since you set your goal:

• What has not turned out as I expected?

• What do I need to keep an eye on?

• What needs my attention right now?

• What (if anything) am I not admitting to myself?

Take the appropriate action to deal with any concerns that these questions highlight before moving on.

This is a quick way to burst out of the "stuck" feeling that can happen when you experience a setback. It helps you to recover your equilibrium, regain your control, and start moving forward again.

1 What stands between you and your next milestone? Identify as many elements of the problem as possible.

2 Take each element and decide whether it is within your power to fix it or not.

3 Decide what you are going to do about each element that you can fix—and do it.

4 Does what is left still stop you from reaching your milestone? If it does, ask for help, or take a different route to get to your goal.

5 Ask yourself what you need to learn from this experience.

it is not. Generally, the longer a problem is left without being dealt with, the more effort it takes to fix. The other drawback to extreme optimism is that it leads to an easily disturbed state of mind. When things do go wrong, it becomes too easy to take it personally, to resent the world for making you suffer, and to look for other people to blame—none of which helps you to solve the problem.

Accept Uncertainty

When you accept that life is not perfect, it becomes easier to see problems coming and prevent them from happening. It also enables you to learn from whatever happens. Once you are confident that you will learn from whatever the future brings, a lot of the reasons for worrying about things going wrong will disappear.

TIP **It is easy to feel good about yourself when things are going well. You show your true character in the strength with which you respond to setbacks.**

Beyond Your Goals

As you move toward your goals, you are also changing yourself. The farther you venture beyond your comfort zone, the more you will learn about yourself and about what it's possible to do in the world.

Look for What Makes You Happy

Research has found that an improvement in material conditions (such as a lottery win or a promotion) brings a temporary increase in happiness, but eventually the recipient's happiness level reverts to around where it started. Only when a gap at the lower levels of the Hierarchy of Needs is filled is there a permanent increase in happiness. Lasting happiness invariably comes from your inner attitude. Your goals may change and evolve as you move toward them, for two reasons:

> **As one set of goals is achieved, the next set emerges**

- because you pick up more relevant information as you move toward your goals.
- because you yourself are evolving.

Work with this—if you had not set your original goals, you would never have found that you can set your sights higher. You may also come up against challenges that you would not have encountered if you had stayed in your comfort zone. You now have plenty of strategies for dealing with them and can tackle them confidently.

Enjoy the Future

What happens when you achieve the goals you have set yourself? This is really a question that only your future self can answer. When you achieve your goals, you will see new challenges and new opportunities beyond anything that you can now imagine—and the only way you will see these wonderful possibilities is to start seriously working toward the goals you have now.

The Hierarchy of Needs

The famous psychologist Abraham Maslow introduced the Hierarchy of Needs model of human motivation, and it is now widely accepted as a pattern in the way in which we work toward our goals.

You read the Hierarchy of Needs from the bottom box upward. The idea behind it is that our goals will be directed toward satisfying these needs in order, starting with the most basic—food and shelter. If someone is homeless, they are unlikely to give much thought to status or self-fulfillment until they have dealt with their most pressing needs. You will notice that the lower levels are driven entirely by "away from" motivation, while the motivation at the highest level has become entirely "toward" the desired goal.

The practical implication that the hierarchy of needs offers for your goal-setting is that you need to make sure the basics are in place before setting yourself more abstract goals. Before setting any goals, carry out some checks to ensure that your finances, relationships, and health are all in good order and working well.

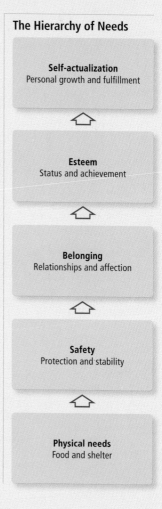

The Hierarchy of Needs

Self-actualization
Personal growth and fulfillment

Esteem
Status and achievement

Belonging
Relationships and affection

Safety
Protection and stability

Physical needs
Food and shelter

Index

Picture Credits

The publisher would like to thank the following for their kind permission to reproduce their photographs: Abbreviations key : (l) = left, (c) = center, (r) = right, (t) = top, (b) = below, (cl) = center left, (cr) = center right.

1: Holger Winkler/zefa/Corbis (l), Reg Charity/Corbis (c), Stephen Toner/Getty (r); **2:** Johannes Kroemer/Getty; **3:** Adrian Turner (t), Creatas/Photolibrary.com (c), Adrian Turner (b); **5:** Peter Cade/Iconica/Getty; **7:** Eric Wessman/Iconica/Getty; **8:** Alt-6/Alamy (l), Ericka McConnell/The Image Bank/Getty (cl), Ghislain and Marie David de Lossy/Getty (cr), Jim Craigmyle/Corbis (r); **13:** © Philippe Royer/ HOA-QUI/Imagestate; **17:** Randy Faris/Corbis; **21:** Adrian Turner; **23:** Ericka McConnell/ The Image Bank/Getty; **27:** Creatas/Photolibrary.com; **28:** Holger Winkler/zefa/ Corbis; **33:** Rommel/Masterfile; **37:** Adrian Weinbrecht/Taxi/Getty; **55:** Matthias Clamer/Getty; **57:** Comstock Premium/Alamy; **67:** Brad Wilson/Iconica/Getty; **69:** Butch Martin/Getty; **73:** Chabruken/Taxi/Getty; **75:** Stephen Toner/Stone/Getty; **83:** Reg Charity/Corbis; **93:** Ghislain & Marie David de Lossy/Getty; **97:** Chuck Elliott/The Image Bank/Getty; **101:** Adrian Turner; **106:** Jim Craigmyle/Corbis; **109:** Eric Wessman/Iconica/Getty; **111:** Colin Hawkins/Getty.

All other images © Dorling Kindersley.

For further information see www.dkimages.com

Author's Acknowledgments

The work of Stephen Covey, in *The 7 Habits of Highly Effective People*, and of Mihaly Csikszentmihaly, in *Flow* was helpful. The P.O.W.E.R. process described in Chapter 4 was originally developed by UK management consultant and coach Jenny Flintoft.

Author's Biography

ANDY SMITH is an emotional intelligence coach and trainer specializing in NLP (Neuro-Linguistic Programming). He has been running the Create the Life You Want workshop for the last ten years, and works with both private and corporate clients, among them Sony, GlaxoSmithKline, and the UK National Health Service. He has written for publications including *The Journal of Primary Care Mental Health* and *The Therapist*. His company, Coaching Leaders Ltd., also runs NLP Practitioner and Master Practitioner training in Manchester, England. Further details are available from www.practicaleq.com. Free downloadable resources to support this book are also available at www.createthelifeyouwant.co.uk.